SIMPLE VAGUS NERVE EXERCISES

50+ PROVEN, EASY-TO-FOLLOW TECHNIQUES TO MANAGE STRESS, REDUCE ANXIETY, AND RELIEVE INFLAMMATION IN JUST 10 MINUTES A DAY

MAX HAMPTON

© **Copyright 2024 - All rights reserved.**

This book is copyright protected. The content contained within this book may not be reproduced, duplicated or transmitted without direct written permission from the author or the publisher, except in the case of brief quotations embodied in critical articles and reviews.. Under no circumstances will any blame or legal responsibility be held against the publisher, or author, for any damages, reparation, or monetary loss due to the information contained within this book, either directly or indirectly.

Disclaimer

The information provided in this book is intended for educational and informational purposes only. The content is not intended to be a substitute for professional medical advice, diagnosis, or treatment. Always seek the advice of your physician or other qualified health providers with any questions you may have regarding a medical condition.

The exercises and techniques described in this book are based on the author's research and personal experience. While every effort has been made to ensure the accuracy of the information, the author and publisher assume no responsibility for errors or omissions. Readers should use their own discretion and consult with a healthcare professional before attempting any exercises or techniques described in this book.

The author and publisher disclaim any liability for any injury, loss, or damage incurred as a result of the use or reliance on the information and techniques presented in this book. The exercises and techniques may not be suitable for everyone, and it is important to consider your own health status and consult with a healthcare provider to ensure that the exercises are appropriate for you.

By reading this book, you acknowledge that you are solely responsible for your health and wellbeing and that the author and publisher are not liable for any adverse effects or consequences resulting from the use of the information provided.

CONTENTS

Introduction	5
1. THE FOUNDATION OF VAGAL TONE	7
Demystifying the Vagus Nerve	8
A Revolutionary View on Well-being	9
The Science of Safety	12
The Key to Emotional and Physical Health	13
Assessing Your Vagal Tone	15
2. THE VAGUS NERVE AND MENTAL HEALTH	19
Anxiety and the Vagus Nerve	19
Fighting Depression with Vagal Tone Exercises	21
PTSD and A Path to Healing	23
Vagus Nerve in Stress Management	25
Enhancing Emotional Regulation	26
3. THE VAGUS NERVE AND PHYSICAL HEALTH	29
The Hidden Link Between Inflammation and the Vagus Nerve	29
The Vagus Nerve's Role in Gut Health	31
Vagus Nerve Stimulation to Combat Chronic Pain	32
Breathing Techniques for Vagus Nerve Activation	35
4. SPECIFIC EXERCISES FOR MENTAL HEALTH IMPROVEMENTS	39
Breathing Patterns to Ease Anxiety	39
Sound and Humming Exercises for Mood Elevation	41
Grounding Techniques for Trauma Recovery	42
Social Engagement Activities to Improve Emotional Regulation	44
Mindfulness and Meditation: The Vagal Pathway to Peace	46
5. EXERCISES FOR PHYSICAL HEALTH CONDITIONS	51
Vagus Nerve Activation for Digestive Health	51
Exercises to Reduce Inflammation Naturally	52

Enhancing Immune Response through Vagal Tone Activities	54
Techniques for Reducing Chronic Pain without Medication	56
Improving Sleep Quality through Vagal Tone Exercises	58

6. DAILY PRACTICES FOR VAGUS NERVE ACTIVATION ... 61
   Quick Morning Routines to Jumpstart Your Vagal Tone ... 61
   Exercises for the Busy Individual ... 63
   Evening Practices for Vagal Tone ... 65
   The Role of Cold Exposure in Vagus Nerve Activation ... 67

7. VAGUS NERVE EXERCISES ... 69
   Breathing Exercises ... 70
   Vagus Nerve Poses ... 105
   Cold Exposure ... 144
   Gargling ... 152
   Progressive Muscle Relaxation ... 156
   Humming ... 161
   Singing ... 169
   Guided Imagery ... 172
   Meditation ... 177

   Conclusion ... 187
   References ... 191

INTRODUCTION

Welcome to a journey towards enhanced health and well-being, one that steers away from conventional medicine and delves into the natural powers of your own body. This book is crafted to shed light on one of the most pivotal yet underappreciated aspects of human health: the vagus nerve. The goal is to transform this complex concept into accessible, actionable knowledge that you can apply to daily life.

Think of the vagus nerve as the unsung hero in your body's story. It plays a critical role in regulating your heart rate, controlling muscle movement, and ensuring your digestive system works smoothly. But its influence extends beyond mere physical functions—it's integral to your emotional and psychological resilience. To help you grasp its importance, imagine it as the body's internal calm button, which you can press to soothe anxiety and reduce stress.

This book is designed to be your guide, written in easy-to-understand language free from medical jargon. Whether you are a health enthusiast or just beginning to explore how your body works, this book is meant to be friendly, encouraging, and empowering.

As we progress, you'll find that this book is structured to take you from a basic understanding of the vagus nerve to a comprehensive set of exercises tailored to stimulate and regulate. This book isn't just another health guide but a practical, detailed directory of every known vagus nerve exercise, each carefully explained and categorized for easy use.

By the end of this book, you'll understand the importance of the vagus nerve and have a toolkit at your disposal. These tools will help you manage daily stress, reduce inflammation, and combat anxiety, enhancing your overall quality of life.

I invite you to approach this book with curiosity and an openness to try new things. Whether you are dealing with specific health issues or simply interested in enhancing your well-being, there is something here for you.

Let's begin this path together, with the promise that understanding and improving your vagus nerve health can lead to significant, positive changes in your life. Let's embrace the potential for transformation, step by step, breath by breath.

CHAPTER 1
THE FOUNDATION OF VAGAL TONE

Have you ever wondered why your heart races when you're frightened or why you get a stomach ache before giving a big presentation? These reactions are part of your body's incredible ability to manage itself without your conscious input, thanks mainly to a remarkable but often overlooked cranial nerve, the vagus nerve. This chapter delves into the fascinating world of the vagus nerve, revealing its crucial role in your body's operations and its potential to significantly enhance your well-being when properly stimulated.

Let's start by exploring what the vagus nerve is and why it deserves much more attention than it typically gets. From controlling your heart rate to influencing your mood and immune response, this nerve is your body's internal highway of communication between your brain and many vital organs. Understanding it is the first step towards harnessing its power to improve your health in ways you might not have imagined possible.

DEMYSTIFYING THE VAGUS NERVE

The vagus nerve, known scientifically as cranial nerve X, is part of your parasympathetic nervous system, often called the "rest and digest" system. Unlike other nerves that might only signal a particular section of the body, the vagus nerve forms a two-way highway from your brainstem down into your belly, touching your heart, lungs, and gut, among other organs. It sends fibers from your brainstem to all the organs that keep you alive and functioning, regulating everything from your heartbeat to your digestion. This extensive influence is why improving the health and tone of this nerve can have such widespread benefits.

Anatomically, the vagus nerve is like the body's superhighway, carrying sensory and motor information that controls bodily functions we seldom need to think about. It originates in the brainstem, just behind the ears, and extends in multiple branches that distribute throughout the thorax and abdomen, sending out various fibers to your organs. These branches are like exit ramps off the highway, directing traffic to the heart, lungs, liver, pancreas, and intestines. The vagus nerve helps regulate heart rate, control muscle movement, manage digestion, and reduce inflammation by releasing neurotransmitters and hormones like acetylcholine, which acts as a brake on inflammation in the body.

The vagus nerve also plays a pivotal role in your psychological and emotional health, acting as the mind-body connection. It is instrumental in calming down the heart and lungs and returning the body to a state of relaxation after stress. This is where the term "vagal tone" comes into play, a term that refers to the activity of the vagus nerve. High vagal tone is associated with a better capacity to relax after stress. In contrast, low vagal tone can lead to more prolonged reactions to stress. Essentially, the better your vagal tone, the more effectively you can manage life's ups and downs.

From an evolutionary standpoint, the vagus nerve is one of the great communicators of the body, having expanded its role and function as vertebrates evolved. Early vertebrates needed the vagus nerve primarily for essential bodily functions like breathing and heart rate. However, as nervous systems became more complex, the vagus nerve took on additional roles, particularly in mammals, including regulating internal organ functions and playing a critical role in social behavior and communication. It's fascinating to consider that our ability to form complex social bonds could be deeply intertwined with the evolution of the vagus nerve, highlighting its importance not just for survival but for thriving in social environments.

This glimpse into the vagus nerve's world shows us that it is not merely a line of communication between the body and brain. It is crucial in our overall health, impacting our physical, mental, and emotional well-being. By learning to improve the tone and health of our vagus nerve, we open a path to alleviate various chronic conditions, enhance our mood, and strengthen our physiological resilience to stress. This understanding forms the backbone of the exercises and strategies discussed in the upcoming sections, aimed at empowering you to take control of this vital aspect of your health.

A REVOLUTIONARY VIEW ON WELL-BEING

Imagine your nervous system as a complex network of highways. Now, envision that within this intricate system, there's a superhighway named the vagus nerve, which we've discussed earlier. Building upon this understanding, let's explore a groundbreaking concept introduced by Stephen Porges known as the Polyvagal

Theory, which has reshaped our understanding of how this nerve influences our social behaviors, stress responses, and overall emotional health.

Introduced in the 1990s, the Polyvagal Theory presents a new way of looking at the body's autonomic nervous system. Traditionally, our autonomic nervous system was viewed as just two parts: the sympathetic (often equated with the 'fight or flight' response) and the parasympathetic (associated with 'rest and digest' states). However, Porges' theory adds a significant layer of nuance by proposing that the vagus nerve is key to a third type of nervous system response that he calls the "social engagement system." This system is unique to mammals and allows us to engage with others when we perceive our environment as safe. It's what enables a mother to calm her crying child with a soothing voice or a smile or allows an individual to build trust in a safe and supportive social setting.

According to Polyvagal Theory, three neural circuits control our bodily state, which can be envisioned as three different lanes on the highway of our nervous system. These circuits are hierarchical, with the most primitive being the sympathetic system. Next is the older dorsal vagal complex, part of the parasympathetic system, which controls more subdued 'shutdown' states, like fainting or freezing, often seen in overwhelming situations. Finally, the newest circuit, the ventral vagal complex, also part of the parasympathetic system, is linked to our social engagement behaviors when we feel safe and relaxed.

This ventral vagal state profoundly influences our feelings of safety and connection. When activated, it helps the body calm down after stress and promotes feelings of calm and trust. This has profound implications for our ability to connect with others. For instance, consider when you felt safe and relaxed in a friend's company, your conversation flowed easily, and you found yourselves sharing and connecting more deeply. This wasn't just good chemistry at play but also your ventral vagal state enabling a safe and engaging interaction.

The practical applications of Polyvagal Theory are vast and varied, stretching across fields such as therapy, education, and personal development. In therapy, for instance, understanding a client's physiological state through the lens of Polyvagal Theory can guide approaches to trauma treatment and anxiety management, focusing on bodily experiences and fostering a state of safety. Educators can apply insights from the theory to create safer learning environments where students are more likely to engage and connect, enhancing their ability to learn and cooperate with others.

Moreover, in everyday personal development, knowledge of the Polyvagal Theory empowers individuals to actively engage their ventral vagal responses to promote feelings of safety within themselves. This can be achieved through practices like deep, slow breathing, social interaction, and even listening to calming music, all of which can help maintain a state conducive to relaxation and positive social interactions.

The beauty of Polyvagal Theory lies in its ability to provide a biological explanation for the interplay between physiological states and emotional experiences. It gives a framework that helps us understand why specific environments make us tense or relaxed, why some relationships make us feel safe and others don't, and how our body's biology is continuously interacting with our emotions and environments to shape our experiences of the world. This understanding demystifies many aspects of human behavior and offers a hopeful perspective on managing stress, cultivating well-being, and improving our interpersonal connections.

THE SCIENCE OF SAFETY

Understanding how our bodies unconsciously assess safety and danger is fundamental to appreciating the profound influence of the vagus nerve on our lives. This process, known as neuroception, describes how our nervous systems distinguish between safe and threatening situations without our conscious awareness. It's not something we think about. It happens automatically, guiding our actions and reactions at a level below conscious thought. Imagine you're walking through a forest. Neuroception allows you to relax and enjoy the beauty around you, sensing safety, as opposed to feeling a sudden chill if you hear a suspicious noise. This automatic scanning of the environment is crucial for survival and is intricately tied to the functioning of the vagus nerve.

The vagus nerve plays a central role as a mediator of safety within this system. The organs it regulates are subtly altered when the body perceives a threat. For example, when a safe environment is perceived, the vagus nerve helps to slow the heart rate, reduce blood pressure, and promote calm and connected states. On the other hand, in dangerous situations, it supports the body in entering a state of heightened alertness, where heart rate and alertness increase, preparing you to fight or flee. This adaptive quality shows how the vagus nerve is directly involved in modulating our physiological state in response to perceived environmental cues.

The impact of this system extends into our social lives as well. A well-toned vagus nerve helps us navigate stress and enhances our interactions with others. When our neuroception detects a safe social environment, it can promote feelings of trust and empathy, making social interactions more rewarding and communication more effective. For instance, consider a scenario where you're meeting someone new. A calm and composed demeanor, supported by good vagal tone, can facilitate a smoother interaction, as your body communicates non-verbal signals of safety and openness to the other person. This can help establish a quick rapport, which is beneficial in both personal and professional settings.

Given the importance of the vagus nerve in shaping our interaction with the world and others, it becomes clear why developing practices to enhance neuroception of safety can be transformative. By learning to regulate its function through deliberate practices, we can enhance our perception of safety, manage stress more effectively, and improve our social relationships. The implications for personal health and social well-being are profound, offering a powerful example of how integrating knowledge about our body's hidden functions can lead to greater health and happiness.

THE KEY TO EMOTIONAL AND PHYSICAL HEALTH

Understanding vagal tone and its significance might just be the key to unlocking better health and a more balanced emotional state. Vagal tone refers to the activity level of the vagus nerve. High vagal tone is associated with better physical and psychological well-being, whereas low vagal tone can lead to various health challenges.

Let's start with how we can measure this elusive yet vital marker of health. One of the most influential and accessible methods is assessing heart rate variability (HRV). This technique measures the time gap between your heartbeats, and these intervals vary when you breathe in and out. High variability indicates that your body can adapt to stress and is generally associated with higher vagal tone. Conversely, low variability suggests lower vagal tone and can be a marker of stress and poor cardiovascular health. Tools to measure HRV range from sophisticated medical instruments to more accessible consumer devices like smartwatches and fitness trackers, making insights into your vagal tone more straightforward.

The implications of having either high or low vagal tone are profound. Individuals with high vagal tone generally enjoy better emotional balance. They can relax more quickly after stress, and their digestion tends to be more efficient, which is crucial as the gut is often called the second brain for its impact on overall health and mood. Moreover, they have a lower risk of inflammatory diseases, heart diseases, strokes, and depression. On the flip side, those with low vagal tone are more susceptible to stress and the diseases it can exacerbate. They might experience mood swings, anxiety, and inflammation and generally have a more challenging time managing glucose levels and blood pressure, which can escalate into more severe health issues.

So, how can one work on improving their vagal tone? Luckily, numerous lifestyle changes and exercises can significantly enhance this crucial aspect of health. Regular physical activity, especially yoga, can increase vagal tone. These exercises focus on deep breathing and relaxation, which stimulate the vagus nerve. Another powerful method is meditation, particularly mindfulness meditation, which has been shown to increase HRV and, by extension, improve vagal tone. Moreover, simple habits like singing, humming, or even gargling water engage the muscles in the back of the throat, which are connected to the vagus nerve, providing gentle, regular stimulation.

Incorporating the practices in the upcoming exercise chapter into your daily routine doesn't just offer the promise of better physical health but also a more serene and balanced emotional life. As you enhance your vagal tone, you may find yourself handling life's stresses gracefully, feeling more connected to others, and enjoying a more profound sense of peace. These changes can significantly impact your quality of life, offering a clear path to manage and thrive in the face of challenges.

ASSESSING YOUR VAGAL TONE

Understanding and measuring your vagal tone is akin to setting the GPS before embarking on a road trip. It tells you where you're starting from, helping you navigate toward improved health and well-being. The process begins with self-assessment techniques that provide a snapshot of your current vagal health, guiding you on the journey to enhance this crucial nerve's function.

One effective way to assess your vagal tone is observing how you react to stress and relaxation. Start by noting your physical and emotional responses to stressful situations. Do you find it difficult to calm down after a stressful event? Do you notice your heartbeat fluctuating during moments of stress and relaxation? These observations can give you clues about your vagal tone. Additionally, paying attention to your digestive system's behavior, such as indigestion or constipation, can provide insights, as the vagus nerve is instrumental in regulating gastrointestinal function.

To better assess your vagal tone, you can use heart rate variability (HRV) as a key indicator. Several consumer-friendly devices and apps available today can measure your HRV, providing you with data that was once only accessible in clinical settings. Using one of these tools, you can regularly monitor your HRV from the comfort of your home. This ongoing monitoring helps assess your current state and plays a crucial role in tracking changes over time, offering a clear picture of how your vagal tone is improving with various exercises and lifestyle changes.

Establishing a baseline for your vagal tone is crucial because it serves as a reference point from which you can measure all future changes, whether improvements or declines. This baseline acts much like a 'before' photo in a fitness program, giving tangible evidence of where you started. To establish this baseline, take consistent HRV readings under similar conditions over several days to account for daily fluctuations. Right after waking up, early morning is a good time for these measurements as it minimizes variables that might affect your heart rate, such as food intake and physical activity.

Once you have established a reliable baseline, interpreting your results becomes the next critical step. If your HRV is on the lower side, it might indicate that you should incorporate more vagus nerve stimulation practices into your daily routine. On the other hand, if your HRV is consistently high, it suggests that your vagal tone is in good shape. However, maintaining and enhancing it through ongoing practices can bring additional health benefits.

Setting realistic goals for improvement based on your assessments is essential. If your initial measurements show low vagal tone, aim for incremental improvements. This could mean setting small, achievable goals, such as increasing your HRV score by integrating specific breathing exercises over a few weeks. Enhancing vagal tone is more like a marathon than a sprint, requiring consistency and patience.

Moreover, it's important to remember that these metrics and self-assessments are tools to guide you, not definitive judgments on your health. They inform and direct your efforts in enhancing your vagal tone, providing a feedback loop that helps you understand your body better and make health decisions that are right for you. This personalized approach ensures that your steps align with your body's unique needs, paving the way for more targeted and effective health interventions.

By regularly assessing your vagal tone, you gain insight into a crucial aspect of your health and empower yourself with the knowledge to make informed decisions about your wellness practices. This proactive approach to health can help you maintain balance, manage stress, and enhance your overall quality of life, keeping you resilient in life's challenges.

CHAPTER 2
THE VAGUS NERVE AND MENTAL HEALTH

Welcome to a chapter that could change how you think about mental health. You can think of your nervous system as a complex control panel, with various buttons and levers regulating everything from your heartbeat to your mood. The vagus nerve is one of the most potent levers within that system, particularly influential in tuning the body's anxiety levels. Understanding the role of the vagus nerve in this context opens up new, natural ways to manage anxiety, potentially reducing the need for medications and their associated side effects. Let's dive deeper into how this remarkable nerve influences anxiety and explore practical ways to activate its calming powers.

ANXIETY AND THE VAGUS NERVE

Anxiety isn't just a feeling. It has a tangible, biological basis involving several body parts, notably the parasympathetic nervous system. The fight-or-flight response is crucial for survival, but when it's constantly triggered by modern-day stressors, it can lead to chronic anxiety. Here, the vagus nerve acts as a counterbalance.

It helps to turn off the fight-or-flight response and initiate a relaxation response, slowing the heart rate and calming the body. When the vagus nerve functions optimally, it can dampen the anxiety response and bring the body back to equilibrium.

Research has shed light on the link between vagal tone and anxiety disorders. Individuals with high vagal tone generally experience less anxiety, as their bodies can relax more quickly after stress. Conversely, low vagal tone is associated with heightened and prolonged responses to stress, which can lead to and exacerbate anxiety disorders. This suggests that improving vagal tone could be a key strategy in managing and potentially reducing anxiety.

Vagus nerve stimulation (VNS) has emerged as a promising method to mitigate anxiety symptoms. VNS involves sending mild electrical impulses to the vagus nerve, activating calming effects. This can be achieved through medical devices or more natural means like specific breathing techniques and physical exercises, which we'll explore shortly. Stimulating the vagus nerve increases the release of neurotransmitters that reduce anxiety, such as acetylcholine and GABA (gamma-aminobutyric acid), fostering a sense of calm throughout the body.

Understanding the direct connection between the vagus nerve and anxiety management and utilizing simple, self-administered techniques to stimulate this nerve can help you take proactive steps toward maintaining a calmer, more balanced mental state. Whether through deep breathing exercises, yoga, or even singing and humming, engaging the vagus nerve can be a powerful tool in your anxiety management toolkit, enhancing your overall quality of life.

FIGHTING DEPRESSION WITH VAGAL TONE EXERCISES

Depression can often feel like a heavy blanket, dulling your emotions and sapping your energy. What if you could lift that blanket using your body's own internal mechanisms? That's where understanding the relationship between depression and the parasympathetic nervous system becomes crucial. This part of your nervous system isn't just about relaxation but is more deeply involved in emotional regulation and mood stabilization.

When the parasympathetic nervous system is out of balance, it can contribute to the symptoms of depression. This imbalance might manifest as a sluggish response to stress, a pervasive sense of sadness, or an inability to experience pleasure. The vagus nerve, which acts as a major conduit in this system, can either exacerbate or alleviate these symptoms depending on its tone. A well-toned vagus nerve promotes a balanced emotional state by regulating biochemicals that affect mood, such as serotonin and dopamine. Conversely, if the vagus nerve's function is diminished, it can lead to a dysregulated state that might contribute to depression.

The good news is that vagus nerve stimulation (VNS) has shown promise in treating depression, especially for those who haven't responded well to traditional treatments. Clinical studies have revealed that targeted stimulation of the vagus nerve can lead to improvements in depressive symptoms. This is likely because VNS helps to restore balance to the parasympathetic nervous system and improves the brain's ability to regulate mood effectively. VNS therapy, which typically involves a device that sends electrical impulses to the vagus nerve, has been FDA-approved for treatment-resistant depression, underscoring its potential as a viable treatment option.

However, not everyone has access to VNS devices, nor is an invasive procedure suitable for everyone. This is where practical vagal tone exercises come into play. These exercises are designed to naturally stimulate the vagus nerve, enhancing its tone and potentially alleviating symptoms of depression. One effective exercise is the easy pose combined with deep breathing in yoga. This pose helps in relaxation and mental calmness, which are beneficial for those suffering from depression. Another technique involves gargling with water, which engages the muscles connected to the vagus nerve, providing gentle stimulation.

Cold exposure can also stimulate the vagus nerve. Ending your shower with 30 seconds of cold water can increase your body's tolerance to stress and improve your mood over time. This might sound daunting, but even a brief exposure can be beneficial. Additionally, singing, humming, or chanting are enjoyable activities that lift your spirits and activate the vagus nerve through vocal cord contact.

Integrating these vagus nerve exercises into your daily routine can be a game-changer for managing depression. The key is consistency and making these practices a part of your lifestyle. For instance, incorporating a few minutes of deep breathing before breakfast, using the cold water technique at the end of your shower, or singing along to your favorite songs during your commute can all be effective ways to enhance your vagal tone throughout the day. These practices help maintain a steady stimulation of the vagus nerve, which can contribute to a more balanced emotional state and potentially reduce depressive symptoms.

By understanding the critical role the vagus nerve plays in regulating mood and incorporating simple, daily exercises that stimulate this nerve, you can actively participate in managing your depression. While these techniques are not a replacement for professional medical treatment, they offer a complementary approach that can help enhance your overall mental health strategy. Remember, small steps can lead to significant changes, and taking control of your body's natural mood regulation system is a powerful tool in combating depression.

PTSD AND A PATH TO HEALING

Understanding trauma and its profound impact on both the mind and body is a complex challenge that has puzzled health professionals for decades. However, Polyvagal Theory offers a fresh perspective, illuminating the pathways through which we might not only comprehend but also address the physiological and psychological repercussions of traumatic experiences. It posits that a well-functioning vagus nerve can help deactivate the defensive states triggered by traumatic events, paving the way for healing and recovery.

Polyvagal Theory elucidates the body's hierarchy of responses when confronted with danger. Initially, our system attempts to deal with threats through social engagement strategies mediated by the myelinated branches of the vagus nerve. If these strategies fail, the body escalates to more primitive mechanisms: fight or flight, controlled by the sympathetic nervous system, and finally, if overwhelmed, to a freeze or shutdown state, managed by the unmyelinated dorsal vagal complex. Traumatic experiences often cause individuals to get stuck in these latter, more primitive, defensive states. The Theory's insights suggest that by activating the more evolved ventral vagal pathways, which promote calm and social interaction, individuals can be guided out of the traumatic freeze response and into a state of safety and social engagement.

The role of the vagus nerve in this process is critical. It acts almost like a brake, helping to regulate and reduce the heightened state of alertness and anxiety that accompanies traumatic memories. When the vagus nerve is stimulated—either through therapeutic practices or lifestyle changes—it can help shift the nervous system from a state of threat to tranquility. This shift is crucial for individuals who have PTSD, as it enables them to move from a hyper-aroused state to one where healing can begin.

In therapeutic settings, various approaches have been designed to leverage the vagus nerve's healing potential. Techniques such as Trauma-Informed Yoga and Somatic Experiencing involve gentle physical exercises and awareness of bodily sensations, which can directly stimulate the vagus nerve, promoting a sense of safety and presence. These methods help re-establish a connection to the body that many with PTSD may have lost.

Building resilience against PTSD is not solely about managing its symptoms but fundamentally about enhancing the body's capacity to engage in life positively. Activities like deep, slow breathing exercises, which increase heart rate variability and signal safety to the brain, are particularly beneficial. Moreover, regular social interaction, which Polyvagal Theory identifies as critical to activating the ventral vagal system, can also fortify emotional resilience. Engaging in community activities, maintaining close relationships, and even pet therapy can provide the social context necessary to stimulate the ventral vagal pathways, promoting feelings of safety and connectedness.

For those dealing with PTSD, incorporating these vagal tone exercises into everyday routines can be profoundly transformative. Over time, these activities not only help alleviate symptoms of PTSD but also contribute to a foundation of emotional resilience, enabling individuals to regain control over their lives and explore a future defined not by trauma but by recovery and hope. This proactive engagement with one's vagal health is a powerful testament to the capacity for change, underlining that recovery is not only about surviving but thriving.

VAGUS NERVE IN STRESS MANAGEMENT

In our fast-paced world, stress is as common as the smartphones in our pockets. As you now know, the vagus nerve is your body's natural calm button, significantly influencing how you handle stress. When you learn to activate and strengthen this nerve, you essentially equip yourself with a powerful tool to manage stress effectively and maintain a sense of peace amidst life's chaos.

Enhancing the tone of the vagus nerve can naturally make your body more resilient to stress. By doing so, you strengthen your body's readiness to perform its tasks to counteract the fight-or-flight triggered by stress. This doesn't just help you feel better momentarily but fundamentally changes your body's response to stressors, making you less likely to get overwhelmed and more capable of bouncing back.

Regular engagement in activities that stimulate the vagus nerve helps maintain a high vagal tone. For instance, deep and slow breathing exercises, which are often instinctive reactions to stress, are scientifically valid methods for stimulating the vagus nerve. When you take a deep breath, your diaphragm sends gentle pressure to the vagus nerve, which then activates the calming response. Daily breathing exercises can significantly enhance your stress resilience, reducing your overall stress levels.

Moreover, incorporating specific vagus nerve exercises into your daily routine can lead to substantial stress reduction. One effective exercise is the 'sphinx pose' from yoga, where you lie on your stomach and prop your upper body up on your elbows. This pose is believed to stimulate the vagus nerve, promoting relaxation.

Another simple technique is to splash cold water on your face immediately after waking up. This action stimulates the vagus nerve by activating the 'diving reflex,' which slows the heart rate and reduces anxiety. Regularly engaging in these activities can strengthen the vagus nerve's ability to manage stress, making you feel more at ease in stressful situations.

Creating a lifestyle that consistently supports vagal tone helps manage stress in the moment while also building a foundation for long-term resilience. By making these practices routine as your morning coffee, you equip your body to handle stress more efficiently and maintain a more relaxed state overall. This shift can have profound implications for your overall quality of life, reducing your risk for stress-related health issues and improving your daily mood. Imagine moving through your days with calm and control, no longer at the mercy of unchecked stress responses. Focusing on strengthening your vagus nerve can become your new reality, transforming how you experience and manage stress daily.

ENHANCING EMOTIONAL REGULATION

Navigating life's emotional landscapes can sometimes feel like steering a boat in stormy seas. Just as calm waters allow clearer navigation, improving your vagal tone can provide a steadier hold over your emotional responses, making it easier to maintain equilibrium even when challenges arise. The vagus nerve, integral to the body's parasympathetic system, is crucial in regulating emotions. By understanding and enhancing its function, you can better manage your emotional life, contributing to improved relationships and overall mental health.

The science behind emotional regulation is deeply intertwined with the vagus nerve's function. This nerve acts like a monitor, assessing and adjusting the body's response to emotional stimuli. When you experience an emotional upset, the vagus nerve helps calm the heart rate and reduce the stress response, which is crucial for returning to a state of emotional balance. This process is known as the 'vagal brake,' where activating the vagus nerve helps slow down the heart rate and enables you to relax faster after getting upset. This is why individuals with a higher vagal tone generally find it easier to bounce back from emotional setbacks—they have a more responsive 'brake system' that allows quicker recovery from stressors.

The link between vagal tone and emotional reactivity is evident in various day-to-day interactions. For instance, if someone cuts you off in traffic, your immediate reaction might be frustration or anger. However, how quickly you can let go of that anger and not let it ruin your day might depend on the tone of your vagus nerve. Improved vagal tone can help you respond to such incidents more calmly and less agitatedly, maintaining your emotional balance despite external stressors.

Now, to actively improve your emotional regulation through vagal tone, there are several exercises you can incorporate into your routine. A beneficial practice is progressive muscle relaxation, which reduces physical tension and subsequently eases emotional stress. This technique involves tensing and then relaxing different muscle groups in your body, which can help trigger the relaxation response of the vagus nerve.

Furthermore, engaging in regular mindfulness meditation can profoundly impact your vagal tone. Mindfulness helps you become aware of your present emotions without judgment, training your brain to remain calm and collected in various situations, which in turn stimulates the vagus nerve. Over time, these practices help manage immediate emotional responses and contribute to a more resilient emotional profile, enhancing your ability to navigate life's ups and downs with greater ease.

The long-term benefits of enhanced emotional regulation are significant. With improved control over your emotions, you'll likely see a ripple effect in various areas of your life, including your relationships and mental health. For example, better emotional regulation can lead to more harmonious relationships, as you're less likely to react impulsively or negatively to those around you. This can enhance your connections with others, fostering stronger, more supportive relationships. Additionally, consistent management of emotional responses can decrease the likelihood of stress-related issues and promote a more positive outlook on life, contributing to overall mental wellness.

As we wrap up this exploration of the vagus nerve's role in emotional regulation, remember that the journey to improved emotional health is ongoing and cumulative. Each step you take builds upon the last, gradually enhancing your ability to face life's challenges with grace and resilience. As we move into the next chapter, we'll focus on the vagus nerve's impact on physical health. We will explore how this mighty nerve influences everything from inflammation to heart health, further underscoring its critical role in our overall well-being.

CHAPTER 3
THE VAGUS NERVE AND PHYSICAL HEALTH

Imagine your body as a finely tuned orchestra, with each instrument playing a vital role in creating a harmonious performance. Now, picture the vagus nerve as the conductor of this orchestra, subtly yet powerfully influencing the players to create a symphony of health. In this chapter, we'll explore one of the most significant roles the vagus nerve plays in our physical health: managing inflammation, which is like the discordant noise that can disrupt the orchestra's beautiful melody if not kept in check.

THE HIDDEN LINK BETWEEN INFLAMMATION AND THE VAGUS NERVE

Inflammation is the body's natural response to injury or infection, a critical part of the healing process. However, when inflammation becomes chronic, it can lead to a myriad of health issues, from arthritis to heart disease and even depression. This is where the vagus nerve steps in, acting through the cholinergic anti-inflammatory pathway. This pathway is a route through which the vagus nerve communicates with the immune system to regulate inflammation.

When activated, the vagus nerve releases a neurotransmitter called acetylcholine, which then interacts with immune cells to decrease the production of pro-inflammatory molecules. So, just like turning down the volume on a loudspeaker, the vagus nerve sends signals to quiet down the inflammatory response. This fascinating connection highlights the nerve's crucial role in maintaining immune balance and positions it as a potential target for therapeutic interventions in inflammatory diseases.

Recent studies have shed light on how the tone of the vagus nerve is inversely related to the levels of inflammation in the body. Higher vagal tone is associated with lower levels of inflammation. For instance, a study published in the Journal of Experimental Medicine demonstrated that individuals with higher vagal tone responded quicker to endotoxins that cause inflammation, indicating a more efficient anti-inflammatory response.

This connection between vagal tone and inflammation suggests that improving the health and function of the vagus nerve can potentially mitigate chronic inflammation. It's a bit like upgrading the conductor of our orchestra, ensuring they're better able to manage any disharmony that arises, keeping the music of our bodies melodious and uninterrupted.

By understanding the crucial role the vagus nerve plays in managing inflammation and enhancing its function through lifestyle changes, you can help maintain your body's harmony. Like a well-conducted orchestra that produces beautiful music, a well-regulated body can lead to a healthier, more vibrant life.

THE VAGUS NERVE'S ROLE IN GUT HEALTH

Have you ever had "butterflies" in your stomach or felt a "gut-wrenching" experience? Such metaphorical expressions are hints at a genuine and complex connection between your gut and your brain, known as the gut-brain axis. This fascinating communication system involves many nerves, hormones, and bacteria that help maintain your overall health. And, of course, central to this communication highway is the vagus nerve

The gut-brain axis is a prime example of how the body's different systems are interconnected. As a significant component of this axis, the vagus nerve plays a crucial role in gastrointestinal health by regulating the release of digestive enzymes. It also helps control the function of the gastrointestinal barrier, which protects your body from harmful bacteria and toxins. When this nerve functions optimally, it ensures your digestive system runs smoothly, like a well-oiled machine, possibly preventing common digestive disorders such as irritable bowel syndrome (IBS) and acid reflux.

Enhancing your vagus nerve's tone can significantly improve your digestive efficiency. This is because a high vagal tone is associated with better control of the digestive process, including faster digestion and more efficient absorption of nutrients. Improved vagal tone also means better regulation of bowel movements, which can alleviate symptoms of constipation and diarrhea. Moreover, a well-toned vagus nerve can enhance the production of stomach acids, which are essential for breaking down food and extracting nutrients.

Stimulating your vagus nerve to promote gut health is straightforward and doesn't necessarily require medical intervention. A helpful practice is mindfulness or meditation, focusing particularly on deep, slow abdominal breathing. This type of breathing can activate the vagus nerve and promote a state of calm in the digestive system, reducing symptoms of gut disorders such as IBS.

The impact of maintaining a healthy gut goes beyond just avoiding discomfort, as it plays a significant role in your overall well-being. The gut is often called the "second brain" because it produces a lot of serotonin. This neurotransmitter significantly affects mood and emotions. A healthy, well-functioning gut can, therefore, improve your mood and mental health, reducing feelings of anxiety and depression. Additionally, since a significant part of the immune system is housed in the gut, maintaining gut health through vagus nerve stimulation can also enhance your immune response, making you better able to fight off infections and diseases.

By understanding the critical role the vagus nerve plays in the gut-brain axis and taking proactive steps to enhance its function, you can significantly improve your digestive and overall physical well-being. As you continue to explore the myriad ways the vagus nerve influences your health, remember that this powerful nerve holds the key to balancing and harmonizing many of your body's critical functions.

VAGUS NERVE STIMULATION TO COMBAT CHRONIC PAIN

Chronic pain is a pervasive issue that affects millions globally, often leading to a significant decrease in quality of life. Pain is a complex interplay of biological, psychological, and social factors, making it challenging to manage. One promising area of research in the battle against chronic pain is the vagus nerve's role in pain perception and management because of its role in modulating pain signals. When you think about pain, it's not just about the physical sensation. It also involves how your brain interprets these signals, and that's where the vagus nerve comes into play.

The connection between the vagus nerve and pain management is rooted in its ability to regulate stress and inflammation—two significant contributors to chronic pain. By influencing the release of neurotransmitters and cytokines, the vagus nerve can modulate pain pathways, potentially reducing the sensation of pain. This modulation occurs through a process known as vagal gating, where the nerve can inhibit or "gate" the pain signals traveling to the brain, preventing the full impact of these signals from being realized. This mechanism suggests that enhancing the function of the vagus nerve could be a key strategy in relieving chronic pain.

Numerous studies have highlighted the effectiveness of vagus nerve stimulation (VNS) in pain management. Research published in various medical journals points to the success of VNS in reducing pain intensity in conditions ranging from migraines to rheumatoid arthritis. For example, a clinical trial found that patients with fibromyalgia experienced significant pain reduction following a regimen of VNS. This is particularly encouraging as it offers an alternative to traditional pain medications, which can have side effects and lead to dependency issues.

Moving from the theoretical to the practical, several VNS techniques can be applied to manage pain effectively. These methods range from non-invasive approaches like transcutaneous VNS, which involves stimulating the vagus nerve through the skin using a small device, to traditional methods, where tiny electrical impulses are delivered directly to the vagus nerve via a surgically implanted device. The choice of method depends mainly on the individual's condition and tolerance for invasive procedures.

For those interested in less invasive options, simple activities like controlled breathing exercises can stimulate the vagus nerve.

Known as "paced breathing," this technique involves breathing at a rate of five to six breaths per minute, significantly slower than the average breathing rate. This slow breathing can enhance vagal activity, promoting relaxation and pain relief. Yoga and meditation also incorporate aspects of this breathing technique and have been shown to improve pain outcomes by enhancing vagal tone.

Integrating these VNS methods into daily life can seamlessly enhance chronic pain management. Establishing a routine with dedicated times for practices like yoga, meditation, or paced breathing can make a substantial difference. For instance, starting the day with a 10-minute meditation session focused on deep, slow breathing can set a positive tone and reduce pain perception throughout the day. Similarly, engaging in a yoga session in the evening can help mitigate the day's stress and pain, promoting better sleep and recovery.

Moreover, regular VNS sessions using a transcutaneous device can be scheduled like any other daily activity, such as taking medications or physical therapy exercises. These devices are typically used for short periods, such as 15-20 minutes twice daily. They can be easily used while reading, watching TV, or working at a desk. The key is consistency. Just as one might take medication at regular intervals, regular use of VNS can help maintain its pain-relieving effects.

By understanding the role of the vagus nerve in pain perception and utilizing VNS techniques, those suffering from chronic pain have a hopeful avenue for relief. This approach helps manage pain more naturally and enhances overall well-being by reducing stress and improving autonomic function, making everyday activities more enjoyable and less painful. Whether through high-tech devices or simple breathing exercises, the potential of VNS in transforming pain management is both exciting and promising, providing a beacon of hope for many who live with the constant challenge of chronic pain.

BREATHING TECHNIQUES FOR VAGUS NERVE ACTIVATION

When you breathe, you do more than take in oxygen and expel carbon dioxide. You also engage a complex interaction between your nervous system and your body's response mechanisms, particularly the parasympathetic nervous system. This system is directly influenced by how you breathe.

Breathing impacts the vagus nerve primarily through its effect on the heart rate and the pressure within your chest. When you take a deep breath, your diaphragm moves downward, increasing the space in your chest cavity and reducing the pressure around your heart, allowing it to expand more fully. This stimulates the baroreceptors, or pressure sensors, in your arteries and heart, sending signals to the brain. The brain responds by increasing vagal tone, slowing the heart rate, and inducing a state of calm. Conversely, when you exhale, and your diaphragm relaxes, the space in the chest decreases, the heart rate picks up slightly, and the activation of the vagus nerve lessens. This natural rise and fall gently massages your nervous system, enhancing vagal tone over time if done consciously and with intent.

One effective method to harness this power is through an intentional breathing technique called the 4-7-8 technique, developed by Dr. Andrew Weil. This technique emphasizes rhythm and control, requiring you to breathe in for 4 seconds, hold your breath for 7 seconds, and exhale slowly for 8 seconds. This maximizes the vagus nerve's response and helps reduce anxiety, improve sleep, and manage stress responses. The extended exhale in this technique is particularly important, as it ensures a more extended period of vagal stimulation, enhancing its calming effects.

Another powerful breathing exercise is alternate nostril breathing, often used in yoga. This involves closing one nostril while inhaling through the other, holding the breath, then closing the first nostril and exhaling through the other. This practice not only focuses your mind, reducing stress and anxiety but also balances the right and left hemispheres of the brain, facilitating a better autonomic and respiratory balance. It's particularly beneficial for the vagus nerve because it encourages a deeper engagement with your breath and a more mindful approach to breathing, both of which enhance vagal tone.

Optimizing your breathing for the best impact on vagal tone also requires attention to how you breathe throughout the day. Most people breathe shallowly, using only the top part of their lungs. This type of chest breathing can keep the body in a low-level state of stress, with less activation of the vagus nerve. To counteract this, focus on diaphragmatic breathing, where the belly expands with each inhale, and contracts with each exhale. This method improves oxygen exchange and maximizes the mechanical stimulation of the vagus nerve, enhancing relaxation and digestive processes.

Incorporating these breathing exercises into your daily routine can profoundly impact your vagal health. Start by integrating short breathing sessions into your morning routine, such as five minutes of 4-7-8 breathing upon waking to set a calm tone for the day. Consider setting reminders on your phone or computer to take short breathing breaks, perhaps a minute of alternate nostril breathing every few hours. This not only breaks the cycle of stress and tension often built up during work but also keeps the vagus nerve engaged and active throughout the day.

By making conscious breathing part of your daily life, you take a decisive step toward better health, leveraging your body's mechanisms to foster calm, resilience, and balance.

CHAPTER 4
SPECIFIC EXERCISES FOR MENTAL HEALTH IMPROVEMENTS

Navigating the complexities of mental health can often feel like trying to find your way through a dense forest without a map. But what if you had a compass that could guide you and help calm your nerves in the process? That's where specific breathing exercises come into play, acting as your navigational tools for enhancing mental well-being. These techniques are designed to directly influence the vagus nerve, helping to ease anxiety, sharpen focus, and restore emotional balance. Integrating these into your daily routine can significantly enhance your ability to manage stress and cultivate a sense of inner peace.

BREATHING PATTERNS TO EASE ANXIETY

Diaphragmatic breathing, often called "belly breathing," is a powerful method that engages the large muscle at the base of your lungs. Unlike shallow chest breathing, which can exacerbate anxiety, diaphragmatic breathing encourages full oxygen exchange and stimulates the parasympathetic nervous system. This technique not only helps reduce stress and anxiety but also improves concentration and stabilizes blood pressure. It acts like a gentle wave, washing over your nervous system and smoothing out the ripples of anxiety.

Extended exhale breathing is a simple yet profoundly effective technique for activating the vagus nerve and enhancing the body's relaxation response. Focusing on making your exhale longer than your inhale helps tip the balance toward parasympathetic activation. This technique not only helps in reducing immediate feelings of anxiety but also contributes to long-term emotional resilience, making it easier to handle stressors as they come.

Box breathing, also known as square breathing, is a technique athletes and military personnel use to enhance focus and calm the nerves. It involves four equal parts: inhaling, holding, exhaling, and holding again. Each step is done to a count of four, forming a "box" of breaths that helps regulate the nervous system. This method not only reduces anxiety but also helps in sharpening focus and increasing mental clarity, making it an excellent tool for moments when you need to center yourself quickly.

Coherent breathing is a technique that aims to bring your breathing rate to about five breaths per minute, which is the optimal rate for affecting heart rate variability and inducing a state of coherence in the body—where the heart, mind, and emotions are in energetic alignment and cooperation. This state of coherence is highly beneficial for reducing anxiety and has been shown to improve cognitive function and emotional resilience. This rhythmic pattern creates a wave-like motion in the nervous system, smoothing out emotional turbulence and fostering a profound sense of calm throughout the body.

Integrating these breathing exercises into your daily life can transform your approach to managing anxiety and stress. Whether starting your day, preparing for a stressful event, or winding down at night, these techniques provide a quick and effective way to restore balance and peace of mind. As you continue to practice and incorporate these patterns into your routine, you may find that not only do your anxiety and stress become more manageable, but your overall sense of well-being also improves, allowing you to navigate life's challenges with greater ease and confidence. Remember, like any skill, the benefits of these breathing exercises are enhanced through consistency and practice, so make them a part of your daily mental health toolkit and watch as they transform your relationship with stress and anxiety, one breath at a time.

SOUND AND HUMMING EXERCISES FOR MOOD ELEVATION

Imagine the gentle hum of a bee or the soothing chants of a choir resonating through a cathedral—these sounds aren't just heard; they're felt. This physical experience of sound, characterized by vibrations, plays a pivotal role in stimulating the vagus nerve. The vibrating nature of sound waves, especially when produced internally through humming or chanting, directly massages the vagus nerve. This stimulation promotes relaxation and can have a profound, uplifting effect on your mood.

The use of humming as a therapeutic exercise is fascinating and incredibly simple to implement. When you hum, the muscles in the face, neck, and chest vibrate, activating the vagus nerve. This reduces the heart rate, lowers blood pressure, and triggers the release of various hormones that create feelings of calm and happiness. Humming doesn't require any special setting or equipment, making it a perfect go-to tool for a quick mood lift wherever you are.

Expanding the scope of vocal exercises, singing your favorite songs can be incredibly therapeutic. Whether it's an upbeat track that gets you dancing or a soft melody that soothes your soul, singing involves similar mechanisms to humming but with an emotional connection to the lyrics and melody. This connection can evoke positive memories and feelings, further enhancing the mood-lifting effects. Singing, particularly in a choir, can deepen your breathing, improve your posture, and offer a sense of belonging and shared emotion, all of which stimulate the vagus nerve. Singing releases endorphins, the feel-good brain chemicals, and oxytocin, a hormone that fosters feelings of trust and bonding.

Incorporating these sound-based exercises into your daily routine can transform your approach to managing mood and stress. They offer a dual benefit: immediate relief from distress through vagal stimulation and long-term mood enhancement through regular engagement in these uplifting practices. So next time you feel the weight of anxiety or sadness, remember that your voice, quite literally, has the power to lift your spirits. Whether you hum or sing, each sound you create is a step toward a happier, more harmonious state of being. As you continue to explore and integrate these practices into your life, you might find yourself not just singing in the shower but using your voice as a powerful tool to master your emotional landscape, one note at a time.

GROUNDING TECHNIQUES FOR TRAUMA RECOVERY

When life throws us into a storm of traumatic experiences, finding our footing can often feel like an impossible task. This is where grounding comes into play, a technique rooted deeply in mindfulness, which focuses on bringing one's attention to the present moment in a non-judgmental way. Grounding techniques are particularly valuable in trauma recovery as they help individuals detach from emotional pain and come to terms with their present environment. These techniques provide a mental "anchor," reducing the occurrence of flashbacks and overwhelming emotions associated with trauma. By learning to ground yourself, you essentially teach your mind and body to reconnect with the present, often leading to a significant decrease in the intensity of traumatic memories.

The effectiveness of grounding lies in its ability to shift your focus from past or future worries to the here and now, engaging your senses to establish safety and stability. This practice can be particularly empowering for those who experience dissociation or heightened anxiety as a result of their trauma. Grounding acts like a bridge, guiding you from a state of heightened alertness—where the world might feel fast and full of threats—to a state of calm presence, where you can manage and process your emotions more effectively. Regularly engaging in grounding exercises helps stabilize mood swings and ensures a gradual reclamation of control over one's emotional responses, fostering a healthier, more resilient nervous system.

The environment around us has a profound impact on our well-being, and this is especially true for those recovering from trauma. Engaging with nature can be a powerful grounding technique, helping stimulate the vagus nerve and promote peace and stability. Simple activities like walking barefoot on grass, gardening, or even sitting by a window with a view of trees can help ground your senses, providing a natural calm often challenging to achieve in urban settings.

Nature's inherent rhythms and patterns have a naturally calming effect on the brain, helping to reduce feelings of stress and anxiety. The sounds of birds singing, the sight of green leaves, or the smell of fresh earth can all serve as natural grounding experiences that bring you back to the present moment and reconnect you with the fundamental joys of being alive. For those living in urban environments, regular visits to parks or natural reserves, or even tending to house plants, can provide a necessary escape and a chance to ground oneself in the calming embrace of nature.

Engaging regularly with grounding techniques can transform your approach to managing trauma and anxiety. They offer practical and accessible tools that help cope with immediate stressors and build a foundation for long-term emotional resilience. By incorporating these practices into your daily life, you open up a path towards healing and recovery, where trauma no longer controls your existence but, instead, where you find strength and stability in the present moment, one step at a time.

SOCIAL ENGAGEMENT ACTIVITIES TO IMPROVE EMOTIONAL REGULATION

Understanding the role of social engagement in emotional regulation can be a game-changer in managing our emotional health. The Polyvagal Theory, developed by Stephen Porges, provides a fascinating insight into how our nervous system interacts with our environment to either calm or distress us. This theory highlights the importance of the vagus nerve in social behavior and emotional regulation. Essentially, when we engage positively with others, our vagus nerve is activated to promote feelings of safety and relaxation. This activation helps to dampen the stress response. It encourages a state of calm, making it easier for us to manage our emotions effectively.

Engaging in social activities can significantly boost this aspect of our nervous system. Activities like participating in group sports, joining a book club, or attending community gatherings not only provide fun and relaxation but also stimulate the social engagement system of our nervous system. This stimulation is crucial for maintaining a balanced emotional state. For example, when you play a team sport, you interact with teammates, communicate strategies, and share in the joy of the game, all of which engage and strengthen the pathways in your brain that promote social behaviors and emotional regulation.

Moreover, these group activities often require cooperation and understanding, which can further enhance your ability to regulate emotions. Engaging in these activities regularly can help build resilience against stress and improve your overall emotional health. The key is consistency, as the more you engage in these social interactions, the stronger and more effective your vagal tone becomes, aiding in better emotional regulation over time.

Another subtle yet powerful aspect of social interaction is the role of non-verbal cues such as eye contact and facial expressions. These elements of communication are powerful stimulators of the vagus nerve. Making eye contact with someone can create a moment of connection that signals safety to your brain, triggering the vagus nerve to calm the body. Similarly, positive facial expressions, such as smiling or nodding, can convey empathy and understanding, strengthening your relationships and enhancing your emotional regulation by activating the vagus nerve.

Creating environments that encourage these kinds of positive interactions is crucial. This can be as simple as arranging seating to face each other in meetings to foster eye contact or setting a norm that encourages smiling and greeting when passing colleagues in the hallway. On a larger scale, designing community spaces that are open and inviting can encourage more frequent and meaningful interactions among community members. These spaces could include community gardens, open park spaces, or community centers designed with comfortable seating areas that invite people to sit, relax, and interact.

In your personal and professional life, strive to create and seek out safe and inviting spaces. This could mean organizing regular meetups with friends or setting up your work environment to encourage open communication and positive interactions. Every small step taken to enhance social engagement can significantly impact your emotional health by leveraging the power of the vagus nerve to foster a sense of safety and connection. Engaging regularly in these activities and interactions isn't just about socializing—it's about actively cultivating a nervous system that supports a calm, happy, and emotionally balanced life.

MINDFULNESS AND MEDITATION: THE VAGAL PATHWAY TO PEACE

In the bustling rhythm of modern life, finding moments of genuine peace can often seem elusive. Yet, the ancient practices of mindfulness and meditation provide us with powerful tools to seek out these moments and fundamentally enhance how our body handles stress and maintains calm. Both practices engage and stimulate the vagus nerve, promoting a relaxation response vital for physical and mental health.

The core principle of mindfulness is simple yet profound: maintaining a moment-by-moment awareness of our thoughts, feelings, bodily sensations, and surrounding environment. This practice particularly benefits the vagus nerve as it shifts the body's focus from stress responses to calm attentiveness. When you practice mindfulness through meditation or even mindful walking, you engage the prefrontal cortex, which activates the vagus nerve, slowing down the heart rate, reducing blood pressure, and facilitating breathing rhythms that promote calm and relaxation. This

SPECIFIC EXERCISES FOR MENTAL HEALTH IMPROVEMENTS

helps reduce stress immediately and bolsters your long-term resilience against stress.

Guided meditation serves as a structured path to achieve this enhanced vagal tone. By following a guided narrative that often incorporates visualization, deep breathing, and body awareness, you can effectively stimulate your vagus nerve. This process shifts your nervous system towards relaxation. It directly engages the vagus nerve, promoting a deep restorative calm.

Body scan techniques further deepen this engagement by sequentially bringing heightened awareness to each part of the body. This method helps develop greater bodily awareness and actively calms the nervous system by signaling safety and relaxation to the brain through the vagus nerve. It's an effective practice for ending your day and preparing your body for a night of deep, restful sleep.

Breath awareness practices are another cornerstone of mindfulness that particularly benefits the vagus nerve. By simply observing the natural flow of your breath—its rhythm, depth, and sensations—you engage a fundamental aspect of your parasympathetic nervous system. This conscious awareness of breathing provides immediate stress relief and strengthens the vagus nerve's capacity to maintain this calm state over time.

As this chapter closes, we reflect on mindfulness and meditation's powerful, simple, and transformative practices. These methods provide immediate relief from the chaos of everyday life and also cultivate a more profound, lasting state of mental clarity and emotional stability. As we transition to the next chapter, we'll explore how these foundational techniques can be applied to managing specific physical health conditions, further illustrating the broad benefits of maintaining a healthy vagus nerve.

UNLOCK THE POWER OF GENEROSITY

"The best way to find yourself is to lose yourself in the service of others."

MAHATMA GANDHI

People who give without expecting anything in return live happier lives. So, let's make a difference together!

Would you help someone just like you—curious about vagus nerve exercises but unsure where to start?

My mission is to make vagus nerve exercises simple, fun, and easy to follow for everyone. But to reach more people, I need your help.

Most people choose books based on reviews. So, I'm asking you to help others by leaving a review. It's free, takes just a minute, and could make a big difference in someone's vagus nerve journey. Your review could help…

…one more person find relief from stress and anxiety. …one more parent feel calm and in control. …one more friend learn how to feel better every day. …one more person improve their health and well-being.

To make a difference, simply scan the QR code or go to the link below and leave a review: https://www.amazon.com/review/review-your-purchases/?asin=B0DH8JNZM7

If you love helping others, you're my kind of person. Thank you from the bottom of my heart!

Max Hampton

CHAPTER 5
EXERCISES FOR PHYSICAL HEALTH CONDITIONS

Imagine your body as a well-tuned orchestra, with the vagus nerve conducting a symphony of smooth digestive processes and robust gut health. In this chapter, we delve into how you can fine-tune this maestro of your nervous system to enhance your digestive wellness and overall vitality. It's about transforming everyday activities into therapeutic moments that nurture your gut, soothe your digestive system, and fortify your body's natural defenses, all through the power of vagus nerve activation.

VAGUS NERVE ACTIVATION FOR DIGESTIVE HEALTH

As well as a digestion center, your gastrointestinal tract is a hub of nerve connections. When the vagus nerve is in optimal condition, it ensures that your digestive processes run smoothly, like a calm and well-navigated sea. However, stress and anxiety can throw this system into disarray, leading to a tumultuous storm of digestive discomfort. This is where gastrointestinal relaxation techniques come into play, acting like skilled sailors who help steady the ship.

One effective method to promote gastrointestinal relaxation is deep, diaphragmatic breathing. This type of breathing engages the diaphragm, which gently massages the vagus nerve with each breath. This exercise not only alleviates stress but also stimulates digestive function by activating the vagus nerve, promoting a smoother digestive process.

Another technique involves progressive muscle relaxation tailored specifically for the abdominal area. Begin by tensing the muscles in your abdomen for five seconds, then release them completely, allowing a wave of relaxation to flow through your digestive tract. This practice can be particularly beneficial after meals or during times of stress, providing immediate relief from cramping and bloating while enhancing overall digestive efficiency.

Yoga, with its emphasis on stretching and breathing, is an excellent practice for stimulating the vagus nerve and supporting digestive health. Specific poses, such as knees-to-chest pose, are particularly beneficial. These poses help relieve gas, ease bloating, and enhance overall digestion by applying gentle pressure to the abdomen, which in turn stimulates the vagus nerve. Integrating these poses into your daily routine can help maintain a rhythmic digestive process and prevent common digestive issues.

EXERCISES TO REDUCE INFLAMMATION NATURALLY

Inflammation is like a fire within your body. It is sometimes necessary as part of the healing process but harmful if it burns unchecked. When activated correctly, the vagus nerve is your body's natural fire suppressant, which is crucial in damping down this inflammation. Engaging this nerve through specific exercises can naturally reduce inflammation, enhancing your overall health without needing medications. Let's explore several techniques that harness the power of the vagus nerve to fight inflammation effectively.

Breathing exercises are a cornerstone of vagal stimulation, directly impacting the nerve's ability to regulate inflammation throughout the body. One effective technique is coherent breathing, which involves breathing at a frequency that maximizes heart rate variability. Over time, this practice helps lower systemic inflammation and promotes a profound sense of calm and control over your body's stress responses.

Another powerful breathing method is the "sigh of relief." This involves taking a deep breath, holding it for a moment, and then exhaling forcefully as if you're sighing. This type of exhale activates the vagus nerve, triggering a relaxation response that can immediately dampen inflammation. Incorporating these sighs into your daily routine, especially during times of stress or after long periods of sitting, can help keep chronic inflammation at bay, protecting your body from the myriad issues that arise from inflammatory conditions.

The therapeutic use of cold exposure, such as ice baths or cold showers, can significantly impact inflammation through vagal stimulation. When exposed to cold, your body initially reacts by increasing blood flow to maintain core temperature. However, as the body acclimates, there's a shift towards parasympathetic dominance, mediated by the vagus nerve. This shift reduces the production of pro-inflammatory cytokines and increases anti-inflammatory markers, helping to control inflammatory responses throughout the body.

To safely incorporate cold exposure into your routine, start with short, controlled sessions. Ending your shower with 30 to 60 seconds of cold water can be an effective way to begin. You can extend the duration or decrease the water temperature as your tolerance increases. Regular cold exposure helps manage inflammation and enhances your overall resilience, improving your body's ability to handle stress and recover from physical exertion.

Stress is a significant trigger for inflammation. When stressed, your body releases hormones and cytokines that can promote inflammatory responses. Engaging in relaxation techniques such as meditation or guided imagery can help turn off the inflammatory cascade initiated by stress. Meditation, in particular, promotes a deep state of relaxation and has been shown to increase vagal tone, which regulates inflammatory processes more effectively.

Setting aside time each day for meditation or guided imagery can substantially affect how your body handles inflammation. These practices help reduce current inflammation and condition your body to manage future stress more effectively, preventing chronic inflammation before it starts. Over time, these moments of calm contribute to a more balanced, inflammation-resistant body, allowing you to enjoy a healthier life with fewer disruptions from pain and illness associated with chronic inflammation.

ENHANCING IMMUNE RESPONSE THROUGH VAGAL TONE ACTIVITIES

The intricate dance between your vagus nerve and the immune system is a fascinating spectacle of biology that underscores the depth of connection within your body. The vagus nerve is pivotal in modulating your body's immune response. This nerve acts like a monitoring system, constantly gauging the health of various body functions and adjusting immune responses accordingly. When the vagus nerve is stimulated, either through specific activities or naturally, it sends out signals that can help regulate inflammation and manage the body's immune reactions. This connection is vital because it means that by enhancing the tone and health of your vagus nerve, you can directly influence and potentially boost your immune system's efficiency.

Regular, moderate exercise is one of the most effective ways to stimulate the vagus nerve and, by extension, support your immune health. Activities such as brisk walking, light jogging, or cycling encourage deep breathing and increase heart rate variability, both indicators of strong vagal activity. These exercises trigger anti-inflammatory responses, which are vital aspects of immune function. They also help in lymph circulation, crucial for transporting white blood cells throughout the body and disposing of toxins and waste. By integrating moderate exercises into your daily routine, you keep your muscles and joints in good shape and fire up your internal defense system, keeping it alert and ready to ward off infections.

Laughter, often dubbed 'the best medicine,' holds more truth than you might realize, especially concerning vagal tone and immune health. When you laugh, your body undergoes several positive changes: muscles relax, stress hormones decrease, and endorphins increase. But more importantly, laughter activates the vagus nerve. Studies have shown that regular laughter can increase the levels of antibody-producing cells and enhance the effectiveness of T-cells, making your immune system more robust. Integrating laughter into your life, whether through social interactions, watching comedies, or even laughter yoga, can be a delightful and effective way to boost mood and immunity.

Social interactions also play a significant role in the health of your vagus nerve and, consequently, your immune system. Positive social encounters stimulate emotional well-being and activate the vagus nerve, which is critical for calming the body and managing stress responses. When you engage in enjoyable social activities, your body increases levels of oxytocin, often referred to as the 'love hormone,' which directly reduces stress and anxiety. Lower stress levels mean less cortisol in the body, which, when elevated, can suppress immune function. Maintaining a vibrant social life filled with supportive and positive relationships is essential to your immune health strategy. By making time for friends and family, participating in group activities, or engaging in community service, you can keep your vagal tone healthy and your immune system robust.

Incorporating these activities into your lifestyle can create a supportive environment for your vagus nerve and immune system, helping you maintain health and vitality. By understanding the deep interconnection between your nervous and immune systems, you can more effectively harness the power of the vagus nerve to enhance your body's natural defenses. Whether through exercise, laughter, or fostering positive relationships, each element contributes to a more resilient you, ready to face whatever challenges come your way. Through consistent practice and awareness, you can turn these activities into powerful tools for health and well-being, keeping your immune system strong and responsive, no matter the season.

TECHNIQUES FOR REDUCING CHRONIC PAIN WITHOUT MEDICATION

Living with chronic pain can often feel like carrying an invisible weight that only you can feel, but managing this pain doesn't always have to mean relying only on medication. There are natural, effective methods that involve stimulating the vagus nerve, which plays a crucial role in controlling the body's pain response. Engaging this nerve through specific techniques can significantly mitigate pain, promoting a more comfortable and manageable life.

Breathing exercises are a cornerstone of pain management through vagal activation. You can dampen the body's pain response when you control your breathing. A particularly effective breathing technique for pain management is the 'paced breathing' method, which involves inhaling slowly through the nose for about five seconds and then exhaling through the mouth for another five seconds. This method helps maintain a rhythmic pattern that optimizes heart rate variability, enhancing vagal tone and reducing pain perception.

Another powerful technique is 'alternate nostril breathing,' a practice borrowed from ancient yoga traditions. This method not only helps focus the mind away from pain but also stimulates different parts of the brain involved in autonomic nervous system regulation, enhancing the body's natural painkilling capabilities.

Yoga is more than just physical exercise because it is a comprehensive mind-body practice that helps reduce pain by enhancing vagal activity. These practices incorporate slow, deliberate movements with controlled breathing, which together help to activate the vagus nerve. For instance, the gentle stretches and poses in yoga help release muscle tension, a common contributor to chronic pain. At the same time, meditative breathing fosters a relaxation response that mitigates pain. Regularly engaging in this practice provides immediate relief from pain and contributes to long-term improvements in managing chronic pain.

Guided imagery is a mental escape that can significantly alter your perception of pain. This technique involves envisioning a specific image, scene, or experience that evokes feelings of calm and happiness, effectively diverting the mind from pain. For instance, imagine yourself on a serene beach, with the warm sun gently bathing your body and the soft sand under your feet. As you visualize these details, your body begins to respond as if you are truly there, which can diminish the intensity of pain.

This technique leverages the brain's powerful role in interpreting pain signals. It uses the mind's capacity to generate soothing, pain-relieving responses. Regular practice of guided imagery can train your brain to more effectively manage the signals associated with chronic pain, making it an invaluable tool for those seeking non-pharmacological pain relief options.

Integrating these techniques into your daily routine can provide a comprehensive approach to managing chronic pain without the reliance on medications. From breathing exercises and yoga to guided imagery, each method offers a unique pathway to pain relief, empowering you to take control of your pain management in a holistic and health-promoting manner. As you continue to explore and practice these techniques, you may find significant improvements in your pain levels and overall quality of life, paving the way for a more active, joyful, and pain-free existence.

IMPROVING SLEEP QUALITY THROUGH VAGAL TONE EXERCISES

Achieving high-quality sleep can sometimes feel as elusive as a dream itself, but by engaging the vagus nerve through specific bedtime practices, you can significantly enhance your sleep quality. One effective way to do this is by incorporating simple vagal stimulation exercises into your nighttime routine. For instance, gentle neck stretches can be particularly beneficial. Slowly tilting your head forward to touch the chin to the chest and then gently rolling the head from side to side activates the vagal nerve fibers in the neck area, promoting relaxation.

Another powerful practice is the 'whispered ah' breathing exercise. As you prepare for bed, sit comfortably and take a deep breath. As you exhale, whisper the sound 'ah,' feeling the vibration in your throat. This exercise not only aids in slowing down your breath but also stimulates the vagus nerve, helping to shift your body into a state of calm readiness for sleep. Doing these exercises regularly as part of your bedtime routine can condition your body to enter a relaxed state more readily, making it easier to fall asleep and improve the overall quality of your rest.

Relaxation isn't just a pleasant state of mind; it's a powerful tool that directly impacts your sleep quality by engaging the vagus nerve. Techniques such as progressive muscle relaxation or deep breathing exercises can significantly activate this nerve, signaling your body that it's time to wind down and prepare for sleep. By focusing on relaxing different muscle groups, starting from the toes and progressing up to the forehead, you engage in a methodical relaxation process that not only eases physical tension but also promotes mental tranquility. This systematic unwinding helps reduce heart rate and blood pressure, both controlled by the vagus nerve, fostering a deeper and more restorative sleep.

As we conclude this exploration of natural and effective ways to enhance sleep through vagal stimulation, remember that consistency is key. Integrating these practices into your nightly routine can transform your sleep quality, contributing significantly to your overall health and well-being. As we move forward into the next chapter, we'll build on these foundations, exploring advanced techniques and lifestyle adjustments that can further enhance your life quality, underscoring the profound impact of the vagus nerve on various aspects of health.

CHAPTER 6
DAILY PRACTICES FOR VAGUS NERVE ACTIVATION

Imagine starting your day not just with a cup of coffee but with a zest that vibrates through your body, setting a tone of calm and control that lasts until you curl back into bed at night. More than just a pleasant thought, this is entirely achievable by tuning into your vagus nerve. Next, we will dive into simple yet profoundly effective morning routines that can jumpstart your vagal tone, ensuring your day begins with an optimal blend of physical and mental well-being.

QUICK MORNING ROUTINES TO JUMPSTART YOUR VAGAL TONE

Your morning sets the stage for the day ahead, and incorporating vagus nerve stimulation techniques can transform this daily routine into a powerful ritual for well-being. Engaging the vagus nerve right after you wake up helps activate your parasympathetic nervous system. This early morning stimulation can help reduce cortisol levels, commonly high in the morning, thereby reducing stress and setting a calm, balanced tone for the day. It's like giving your body a preview of the peace and stability it can experience throughout the day, encouraging a more harmonious rhythm between your body's biological systems.

One of the most effective and easiest ways to stimulate the vagus nerve is through deep, slow breathing exercises. With an exercise called diaphragmatic breathing, you aim to take six breaths per minute, typically inhaling for five seconds and exhaling for five seconds. This practice helps reduce stress and anxiety and optimizes heart function and blood pressure regulation throughout your day.

Another quick exercise is the Valsalva maneuver. Take a deep breath and try to exhale while keeping your mouth and nose closed. This creates pressure in your chest and stimulates the vagus nerve. Performing this maneuver a couple of times can increase vagal tone and improve heart rate variability, making you more resilient to stress.

Incorporating these vagal activation techniques into your morning routine can enhance their benefits and ensure they become a seamless part of your day. For instance, while waiting for your coffee to brew or after brushing your teeth, take a few minutes to engage in breathing exercises. This ensures consistency and makes it easier to turn these exercises into a habit. You can also pair vagal exercises with morning stretches or light yoga poses to further enhance blood flow and relaxation, preparing your mind and body for the day ahead.

Starting your day with focused vagus nerve stimulation can have immediate and long-term benefits. In the short term, it helps to clear your mind, lower your stress levels, and increase your energy by improving your sleep quality and mood. In the long term, regular morning vagal activation can strengthen your immune system, enhance your digestive health, and reduce the risk of heart-related issues. It's a compound effect—the more consistently you perform these exercises, the more pronounced their benefits become, leading to a healthier, more vibrant life.

EXERCISES FOR THE BUSY INDIVIDUAL

Maintaining your vagal tone isn't just a morning or evening task but a continuous commitment that extends even into your busiest workdays. The stress and fast pace of modern work life can often lead your body into a state of sympathetic dominance, where fight or flight responses become frequent. However, incorporating simple vagus nerve activation practices into your workday can significantly enhance your resilience to stress, maintain your focus, and boost your overall well-being. These practices are designed to be subtle yet effective, ensuring that you can remain centered and calm even during the most hectic days.

For many, the idea of exercising at the office or during work might seem impractical or distracting. However, you can perform several discreet yet powerful exercises without ever leaving your desk. One of the simplest methods is the 'Sigh of Relief.' This involves taking a deep breath, holding it for a moment, and then exhaling slowly through your mouth with a sigh. This exercise can be a quick reset for your nervous system, especially before entering a stressful meeting or tackling a challenging task. Another minimally disruptive practice is to slightly adjust the 'cat-cow stretch' to be performed in a chair, which involves sitting with your hands on your knees and alternately arching and rounding your back. This movement not only eases tension in the spine and neck but also stimulates the vagus nerve by encouraging deep, focused breathing.

Your lunch break is perfect for stepping up your vagus nerve activation practices. Most people use this time to eat or catch up on personal tasks, but it's also an ideal moment to engage in practices that enhance your vagal tone. A brief walk outside, for instance, can do wonders. Physical activity and exposure to natural light and fresh air stimulate the vagus nerve while reducing stress hormones. If a walk isn't possible, find a quiet space to practice a few minutes of guided relaxation or meditation.

Posture and movement throughout the day play significant roles in maintaining vagal tone. Poor posture, often exacerbated by long periods of sitting, can compress the abdominal region, restricting the diaphragm and impeding the optimal function of the vagus nerve. To counter this, make a conscious effort to maintain a posture that supports deep breathing. Ensure that your back is straight, your shoulders are relaxed, and your chest is open. Take a moment to stand up, stretch, and adjust your posture every hour. Simple neck rolls or shoulder shrugs relieve tension and activate the vagus nerve by involving the neck muscles, where it is extensively branched.

Integrating these practices into your daily routine at work doesn't require dramatic changes to your schedule. Instead, it's about making minor adjustments that can be seamlessly incorporated into your existing routines. By setting regular reminders to take deep breaths, stretch, or walk, these activities can become second nature, enhancing your productivity and well-being without disrupting your workflow. Over time, these small practices accumulate, leading to significant improvements in your stress levels, focus, and overall health. They allow you to harness the power of the vagus nerve to not only survive but thrive in your busy work environment, turning ordinary days into opportunities for growth and well-being.

EVENING PRACTICES FOR VAGAL TONE

As the sun sets and the pace of the day begins to slow, it's the perfect time to focus on calming the body and preparing for restorative sleep. The evening is a critical period for engaging in practices that promote relaxation and enhance vagal tone, setting the stage for a deep, restful sleep. This natural winding down aligns perfectly with the body's nocturnal rhythms, making it an ideal time to engage the vagus nerve to activate your body's relaxation responses.

One of the most soothing ways to enhance vagal tone in the evening is through guided relaxation techniques that involve visualization and progressive muscle relaxation. This can be done by lying down in a quiet, comfortable space and slowly tensing and relaxing each muscle group, starting from the toes and moving upwards to the crown of the head. As you focus on releasing tension from your body, your mind follows, allowing the vagus nerve to facilitate a deeper state of calm. Complement this practice with deep, rhythmic breathing to further activate the vagus nerve, encouraging it to slow the heart rate and lower blood pressure, easing the body into a state of relaxation.

Adding a layer to this routine with aromatherapy can significantly enhance the calming effects. Scents like lavender, chamomile, or sandalwood can be used in an oil diffuser or applied as essential oils to pressure points on the body. These scents provide a soothing atmosphere and stimulate the olfactory system, which is directly linked to the areas of the brain that control emotions and the autonomic nervous system, thereby supporting the relaxation facilitated by vagal stimulation.

Combining vagal stimulation with relaxation techniques such as meditation and gentle yoga in the evening creates a powerful synergy that enhances the effects of each practice. Gentle yoga sequences designed for nighttime can include poses such as 'Legs-Up-the-Wall' or gentle spinal twists, which release physical tension, encourage deeper breathing, and engage the parasympathetic nervous system. Following up your yoga practice with meditation can further deepen the relaxation response. Techniques like mindfulness meditation or mantras can focus and calm the mind, reducing stress and anxiety and making it easier for the vagus nerve to induce relaxation.

The transition from yoga to meditation can be seamless. For example, the final pose of your yoga practice might evolve into a seated or lying meditation position. This not only makes the routine fluid but also helps maintain the relaxed state achieved through yoga without disruption. Integrating these practices at the end of your day enhances your immediate sense of calm and contributes to long-term improvements in vagal tone.

Another simple yet effective technique is the 'humming bee breath,' which involves humming during exhalation. This practice generates a natural vibration in the body, which is felt most prominently in the face and head, areas rich in vagus nerve endings. The vibration stimulates the nerve, promoting relaxation and sleepiness. Performing this exercise in bed before sleep creates a soothing end to your day and signals your brain to prepare for deep sleep.

Incorporating these practices into your evening routine helps you unwind effectively and sets a natural rhythm that your body begins to recognize, making it easier to transition into relaxation and sleep over time. This routine acts like a signal to your body, indicating that it's time to shift gears from the day's activities to night's rest, enhancing your overall sleep quality and contributing to better health and well-being.

THE ROLE OF COLD EXPOSURE IN VAGUS NERVE ACTIVATION

Imagine stepping into a brisk, cold shower or dipping your face into a bowl of ice-cold water. While it might sound shockingly uncomfortable, this practice of cold exposure is a scientifically backed method to stimulate your vagus nerve. The initial shock of the cold triggers a flood of responses in your body that ultimately lead to significant health benefits, particularly in improving the tone and function of the vagus nerve.

The science behind cold therapy, or cryotherapy, reveals fascinating insights into how our bodies respond to extreme cold. When exposed to cold, your body initially reacts with a fight-or-flight response, including an increased heart rate and blood pressure. However, this is quickly followed by a parasympathetic response. This shift helps decrease your heart rate and increase your vagal tone, which is crucial for calming the body after stress. Moreover, cold exposure has been shown to increase levels of norepinephrine, a neurotransmitter that can help improve focus, increase energy levels, and reduce pain. This cascade of physiological effects not only boosts mood and energy but also strengthens the body's ability to handle stress and recover from physical exertion.

Practicing cold exposure safely is crucial to reap its benefits without risking harm. It's important to start gradually and listen to your body's reactions. For beginners, ending a regular warm shower with 30 seconds of cold water can be a good start. This brief exposure can invigorate the body without causing undue stress. As you become more accustomed to the sensation, you can slowly increase the duration and frequency of cold exposure.

Integrating cold exposure into your daily wellness routine can be surprisingly manageable. If morning showers are part of your routine, switching the last minute to cold water is a simple yet effective way to stimulate the vagus nerve and wake up your body. For those who exercise regularly, a brief cold shower post-workout can enhance muscle recovery by reducing inflammation and boosting vagal tone, aiding in quicker physiological recovery. For an invigorating start to your day, try splashing your face with cold water after waking up. This can sharpen your alertness and calm your nerves, preparing you for the day's challenges.

Consistently incorporating these practices can lead to long-term improvements in your vagal tone, resilience to stress, and overall energy levels. While the initial discomfort may deter some, the invigorating and rejuvenating effects of cold exposure are worth the brief chill. Over time, as your body adapts, these practices may become an essential and enjoyable part of your wellness routine, offering a refreshing boost to both your physical and mental health.

CHAPTER 7
VAGUS NERVE EXERCISES

In this chapter, we embark on a practical journey to explore the diverse and effective exercises designed to stimulate the vagus nerve, which can be activated through a variety of techniques, each offering unique benefits. Here, we will provide detailed, step-by-step instructions for various exercises, including specialized breathing methods, poses tailored for nerve activation, the often-overlooked practice of gargling, progressive muscle relaxation techniques, the calming hum, and many others. These exercises are routines and gateways to enhancing your body's natural healing processes. Prepare to dive into a world of simple yet powerful practices that can be seamlessly integrated into your daily life, promoting resilience and a profound sense of well-being.

BREATHING EXERCISES

Tips for Effective Breathing Practice

Practice Regularly:

- Practice a breathing exercise routine daily, even if just for a few minutes, to build the habit and experience its benefits.

Create a Quiet Environment:

- If possible, eliminate distractions during the exercise. This helps you concentrate on the experience and enhances the relaxation benefits.

Stay Patient:

- Be gentle with yourself and allow the practice to develop naturally. Avoid forcing the breath; let it come naturally.

Combine with Meditation:

- Pair breathing with meditation or mindfulness practices to deepen relaxation and enhance vagus nerve stimulation.

Use Visualization:

- Imagine a peaceful scene or visualize the air flowing in and out of your body to enhance relaxation.

Use a Timer:

- Set a timer to help you keep track of the time and stay focused on your breathing without worrying about the clock.

Benefits of Breathing Practice

Stimulates the Vagus Nerve:

- The combination of deep breathing and forceful or focused exhalation activates the parasympathetic nervous system, promoting relaxation and reducing stress.

Reduces Anxiety and Stress:

- Helps manage anxiety and stress by calming the mind and body.

Promotes Overall Relaxation:

- Encourages a state of calm and well-being.

Releases Tension:

- Helps to physically and mentally release built-up tension.

Enhances Mindfulness:

- Brings awareness to the present moment and improves concentration.

Breathing Exercise First Steps

Find a Comfortable Position:

- Select a quiet, comfortable place to sit or lie down without disturbances. If you are sitting, keep your back straight and shoulders relaxed. If you are lying down, rest comfortably on your back with your arms by your sides.

Relax Your Body:

- Close your eyes to minimize distractions. Take a moment to relax your body, releasing any tension in your shoulders, neck, and jaw.

Mindful Awareness:

- Focus on the sensations of your breath as it enters and leaves your body. If your mind wanders, gently bring it back to your breathing.

Deep Relaxation:

- Allow the breathing to bring a sense of calm and relaxation. Visualize each breath bringing in relaxation, and each exhale releasing tension.

Ending Your Breathing Exercise

Ease Out:

- After completing the desired duration, gradually return to your regular, relaxed breathing pattern. Take a few deep breaths at your own pace.

Notice Changes:

- Reflect on how you feel after the exercise. Notice any changes in your stress or anxiety levels and acknowledge the sense of calm and presence.

Post-Exercise Relaxation:

- Take a moment to sit quietly and integrate the relaxation and calmness you have cultivated.

Unless exercises specifically direct otherwise, follow these steps at the beginning and end of every exercise for the most effective experience.

* * *

Lion's Breath

Lion's Breath is a breathing technique that involves forceful exhalation and a roaring sound.

1. Inhale Deeply:

- Breathe in slowly and deeply through your nose, filling your lungs completely. Allow your abdomen to rise as you inhale.

2. Exhale Slowly:

- Exhale slowly through your mouth, feeling your body relax with each breath. Repeat this deep breathing for 1-2 minutes to prepare for the Lion's Breath exercise.

3. Inhale Deeply:

- Take a deep breath in through your nose, filling your lungs completely.

4. Exhale Forcefully with a Roaring Sound:

- Open your mouth wide, stick out your tongue as far as possible towards your chin, and exhale forcefully through your mouth, making a "ha" sound that comes from deep within your diaphragm.
- As you exhale, focus on the tip of your nose or look between your eyebrows.

5. Repeat the Process:

- After the first breath, close your mouth and take another deep breath in through your nose. Repeat the forceful exhalation with the "ha" sound for 5-10 breaths.

6. Duration:

- Practice Lion's Breath for 1-3 minutes, or as long as feels comfortable. Maintain a steady and relaxed rhythm, focusing on the breath and the calming effect.

7. Stay Relaxed:

- Pay attention to how your body feels as you continue the Lion's Breath. Notice the relaxation spreading through your body with each breath.

* * *

Pursed Lip Breathing

Pursed lip breathing is a simple and effective technique that involves inhaling through the nose and exhaling through pursed lips. This practice helps to improve ventilation, reduce shortness of breath, and promote relaxation.

1. Breathe Normally:

- Take a normal breath in through your nose, filling your lungs comfortably without straining.

2. Inhale Deeply:

- Breathe in slowly and deeply through your nose for about 2 seconds. Allow your abdomen to rise as you inhale.

3. Lip Position:

- Pucker or purse your lips as if you are going to whistle or blow out a candle. This should create a small opening for the air to pass through.

4. Exhale Slowly:

- Exhale slowly and gently through your pursed lips for about 4 seconds, making the exhalation twice as long as the inhalation. Focus on making the exhalation steady and controlled.

5. Repeat the Process:

- Continue the cycle of inhaling deeply through your nose for 2 seconds and exhaling slowly through your pursed lips for 4 seconds. Maintain a steady and relaxed rhythm.

6. Duration:

- Practice pursed lip breathing for 5-10 minutes, or as long as feels comfortable. Maintain a steady and relaxed rhythm, focusing on the breath and the calming effect.

7. Stay Relaxed:

- Pay attention to how your body feels as you continue the pursed lip breathing. Notice the relaxation spreading through your body with each breath.

* * *

Cooling Breath

Cooling breath is a breathing technique that helps to cool the body, calm the mind, and promote relaxation. This practice involves inhaling through a rolled tongue and exhaling through the nose.

1. Tongue Position:

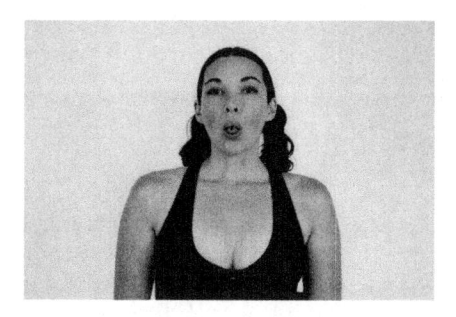

- Curl the sides of your tongue to form a tube or straw-like shape. If you cannot curl your tongue, simply place your tongue between your teeth and lips, making a small "o" shape with your lips.

2. Take Deep Breaths:

- Breathe in slowly and deeply through your nose, filling your lungs completely. Allow your abdomen to rise as you inhale.

3. Inhale Through Your Rolled Tongue:

- Stick out your rolled tongue and inhale deeply through the tube formed by your tongue. Feel the cool air entering your mouth and traveling into your lungs.

4. Close Your Mouth and Exhale Through Your Nose:

- After a full inhalation, close your mouth and exhale slowly and fully through your nose. Focus on making the exhalation steady and controlled.

5. Repeat the Process:

- Continue the cycle of inhaling through your rolled tongue and exhaling through your nose. Maintain a steady and relaxed rhythm.

6. Duration:

- Practice Cooling Breath for 5-10 minutes, or as long as feels comfortable. Maintain a steady and relaxed rhythm, focusing on the breath and the calming effect.

7. Stay Relaxed:

- Pay attention to how your body feels as you continue the Cooling breath. Notice the relaxation spreading through your body with each breath.

* * *

Deep Sigh Breathing

Deep Sigh Breathing is a simple yet effective technique that involves deep, intentional sighs to release tension, promote relaxation, and stimulate the vagus nerve.

1. Inhale Deeply:

- Take a deep breath in through your nose, filling your lungs completely and allowing your chest and abdomen to expand.

2. Sigh Out Loud:

- Exhale through your mouth with an audible sighing sound. Make the sigh long and drawn out, allowing your shoulders and body to relax fully as you release the breath.

3. Repeat the Sigh:

- After the first sigh, immediately take another deep breath in through your nose.
- Exhale again through your mouth with an audible sigh, similar to the first one. Focus on releasing any remaining tension in your body.

4. Deep Breathing:

- Take slow, deep breaths between each set of sighs. Inhale deeply through your nose and exhale slowly through your mouth.

5. Continue for Several Minutes:

- Repeat the Deep Sigh Breathing process for 5-10 minutes, or as long as feels comfortable. Maintain a steady and relaxed rhythm, focusing on the release of tension and the calming effect.

6. Stay Relaxed:

- Pay attention to how your body feels after each sigh. Notice the relaxation spreading through your body with each breath and sigh.

* * *

Breath Counting

Breath counting is a mindfulness technique that involves counting each breath to help focus the mind, reduce stress, and stimulate the vagus nerve.

1. Deep Breathing:

- Breathe in slowly and deeply through your nose, filling your lungs completely. Allow your abdomen to rise as you inhale.

- Exhale slowly through your mouth, feeling your body relax with each breath. Repeat this deep breathing for 1-2 minutes to prepare for the breath counting exercise.

2. Start Counting Your Breaths:

- As you inhale, count silently to yourself, "one."
- As you exhale, count silently to yourself, "two."

3. Continue Counting:

- On the next inhale, count silently "three."
- On the next exhale, count silently "four."

4. Count to Ten:

- Continue this pattern of counting each inhale and exhale up to ten. For example, inhale "five," exhale "six," inhale "seven," exhale "eight," inhale "nine," and exhale "ten."

5. Start Over at One:

- After reaching ten, start the counting cycle over at one.

6. Duration:

- Practice breath counting for 5-10 minutes, or as long as feels comfortable. Maintain a steady and relaxed rhythm, focusing on the counting and the calming effect.

7. Stay Relaxed:

- Pay attention to how your body feels as you continue counting breaths. Notice the relaxation spreading through your body with each breath.

* * *

Ocean Breath

Ocean Breath is a breathing technique that involves gently constricting the throat to create a soothing sound, similar to ocean waves.

1. Deep Breathing:

- Breathe in slowly and deeply through your nose, filling your lungs completely. Allow your abdomen to rise as you inhale.
- Exhale slowly through your nose, feeling your body relax with each breath. Repeat this deep breathing for 1-2 minutes to prepare for the Ocean Breath.

2. Slight Constriction:

- Slightly constrict the back of your throat as if you were whispering or fogging up a mirror. This constriction creates a soft, ocean-like sound as you breathe.

3. Mouth Closed:

- Keep your mouth closed and breathe in and out through your nose, maintaining the gentle constriction in your throat.

4. Inhale with Sound:

- Inhale slowly and deeply through your nose, creating a soft, ocean-like sound as the air passes through the constricted throat. Focus on a steady and even inhalation.

5. Exhale with Sound:

- Exhale slowly and fully through your nose, maintaining the ocean-like sound. Ensure the exhalation is steady and controlled.

6. Maintain the Rhythm:

- Continue the cycle of inhaling and exhaling with the ocean breath sound. Aim for a smooth and continuous rhythm, with each breath lasting for several seconds.

7. Duration:

- Practice Ocean Breath for 5-10 minutes, or as long as is comfortable. Maintain a steady rhythm and focus on the relaxation it brings.

Whispered "Ah" Breathing

This exercise involves deep breathing combined with gentle vocalization, which can help activate the parasympathetic nervous system.

1. Inhale Deeply:

- Take a deep breath in through your nose, allowing your abdomen to rise and your lungs to fill completely.

2. Hold the Breath Briefly:

- Hold the breath for 2-3 seconds to let the oxygen circulate and to prepare for the exhalation.

3. Exhale with a Whispered "Ah":

- As you exhale, make a gentle "ah" sound. Like a gentle whisper, the sound should be soft, smooth, and continuous. Focus on making the sound as calm and soothing as possible.
- Ensure the "ah" sound is soft and gentle. Avoid straining your vocal cords. The sound should be soothing and relaxed.

4. Focus on the Sensation:

- Pay attention to the vibration and sensation in your throat and chest as you make the "ah" sound. Notice how the sound and the exhalation help to relax your body.

5. Continue the Cycle:

- Repeat the cycle of inhaling deeply, holding the breath briefly, and exhaling with a whispered "ah" sound. Aim for 5-10 repetitions, maintaining a steady, relaxed breathing pattern.

6. Maintain Relaxation:

- Continue to take slow, deep breaths throughout the exercise. With each inhale, imagine drawing in relaxation and calm; with each exhale, release any tension or stress.

* * *

Sigh of Relief Exercise

This exercise mimics the body's natural sigh response, which can help release tension and induce a sense of calm.

1. Take a Deep Inhale

- Breathe in slowly and deeply through your nose, filling your lungs completely. Allow your abdomen to rise as you fill your lungs with air.

2. Hold Your Breath Briefly

- Hold your breath for a count of 2-3 seconds. This brief pause allows your body to absorb the oxygen fully.

3. Exhale with a Sigh

- Exhale slowly and completely through your mouth, making a gentle sighing sound as you release the air. Allow your shoulders to drop and your body to relax as you sigh.
- Ensure your sighs are gentle and relaxed, not forced. The goal is to release tension and promote calmness.

4. Focus on the Sensation

- Pay attention to the sensation of relaxation that follows the sigh. Feel the tension leaving your body and a sense of calm taking over.

5. Repeat the Cycle

- Repeat the cycle of deep inhaling, holding, and sighing out for 5-10 minutes. Maintain a steady rhythm and focus on the relaxation with each sigh.

6. End with Deep Breathing

- After completing the sighing cycles, take a few final deep breaths at your own pace. Inhale deeply through your nose and exhale slowly through your mouth.

Humming Bee Breath

1. Position Your Hands:

- Place your thumbs gently on your ear cartilage (the flap covering the ear canal). Your other fingers can rest on your forehead or gently cover your eyes.

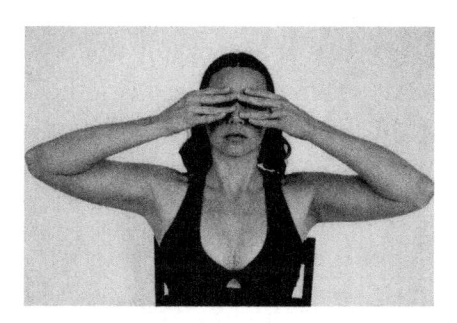

2. Inhale Deeply:

- Take a deep breath in through your nose, filling your lungs completely.

3. Exhale with a Humming Sound:

- As you exhale, make a gentle humming sound, like the sound of a bee. Keep your mouth closed and feel the vibration in your throat and head.
- Try to extend the exhalation and the humming sound as long as it is comfortable without straining.
- Pay attention to the humming sound and its vibration. This mindfulness aspect enhances the calming effect.

4. Focus on the Vibration:

- Focus on the soothing vibration created by the humming sound. This vibration helps stimulate the vagus nerve and promotes relaxation.

5. Repeat the Process:

- Continue the Practice: Inhale deeply again through your nose and repeat the humming sound on the exhale. Continue this cycle for 5-10 minutes.

6. End with Deep Breathing:

- Complete the Practice: After completing the cycles of Bhramari Pranayama, take a few final deep breaths through your nose. Notice the sense of calm and relaxation.

* * *

Extended Exhale Breathing

1. Hand Placement:

- Place one hand on your belly and the other on your chest. This will help you feel the movement of your breath and ensure you are breathing deeply into your belly.

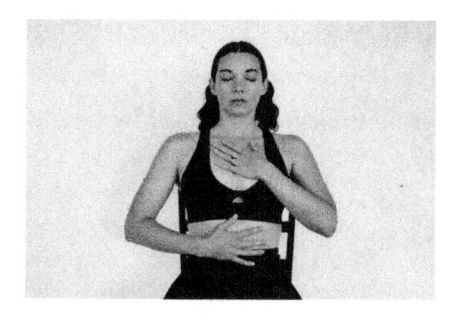

2. Inhale Slowly and Deeply:

- Breathe in slowly through your nose for a count of 4. Feel your abdomen rise as you fill your lungs with air. Your chest should remain relatively still.

3. Pause Briefly:

- Gently hold your breath for 1-2 seconds. This brief pause allows your body to fully absorb the oxygen.

4. Exhale Slowly and Completely:

- Exhale slowly and completely through your mouth or nose for a count of 6-8. Focus on making your exhalation longer than your inhalation. Feel your abdomen fall as you release the air.

5. Continue the Cycle:

- Continue this cycle of breathing: inhale for 4 counts, hold for 1-2 counts, and exhale for 6-8 counts. Aim to practice for 5-10 minutes.

6. End with Deep Breathing:

- After completing the cycles, take a few final deep breaths at your own pace. Notice how your body feels more relaxed and your mind calmer.

* * *

Box Breathing

1. Visualize a Box:

- Imagine a box with four equal sides. Each side represents a part of the breathing cycle: inhale, hold, exhale, and hold.

2. Inhale Slowly and Deeply:

- Breathe in slowly through your nose for a count of 4. Fill your lungs completely, allowing your abdomen to rise.

3. Hold Your Breath:

- Gently hold your breath for a count of 4. This pause allows your body to fully absorb the oxygen.

4. Exhale Slowly and Completely:

- Exhale slowly and completely through your mouth for a count of 4. Feel your abdomen fall as you release the air.

5. Hold Your Breath Again:

- After exhaling, hold your breath again for a count of 4. This second pause helps to reset your breathing cycle.

6. Repeat the Cycle:

- Continue this cycle of breathing: inhale for 4 counts, hold for 4 counts, exhale for 4 counts, and hold for 4 counts. Aim to practice for 5-10 minutes.

7. End with Deep Breathing:

- After completing the cycles, take a few final deep breaths at your own pace. Notice how your body feels more relaxed and your mind calmer.

* * *

Coherent Breathing

Coherent breathing, also known as resonant breathing, involves breathing at a steady rate that maximizes heart rate variability and stimulates the vagus nerve. It is a powerful technique for reducing stress and promoting relaxation.

1. Inhale Slowly and Deeply:

- Breathe in slowly and deeply through your nose for a count of 5-6. Fill your lungs completely, allowing your abdomen to rise.

2. Exhale Slowly and Completely:

- Exhale slowly and completely through your nose for a count of 5-6. Feel your abdomen fall as you release the air.

3. Continue the Cycle:

- Continue this cycle of breathing: inhale for 5-6 counts and exhale for 5-6 counts. Aim to practice for 10-20 minutes.

4. Focus on Your Breathing:

- Maintain your focus on the rhythm of your breath and the sensation of relaxation. If your mind wanders, gently bring it back to your breath.

5. End with Deep Breathing:

- After completing the cycles, take a few final deep breaths at your own pace. Notice how your body feels more relaxed and your mind calmer.

* * *

Paced Breathing

1. Hand Placement:

- Place one hand on your belly and the other on your chest. This will help you feel the movement of your breath and ensure you are breathing deeply into your belly.

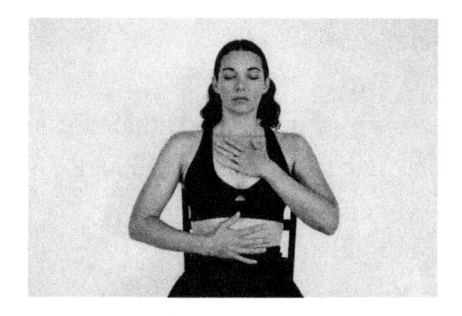

2. Inhale Slowly and Deeply:

- Breathe in slowly through your nose for a count of 4. Feel your abdomen rise as you fill your lungs with air. Your chest should remain relatively still.

3. Hold Your Breath:

- Gently hold your breath for a count of 4. This brief pause allows your body to fully absorb the oxygen.

4. Exhale Slowly:

- Exhale slowly and completely through your mouth for a count of 6. Feel your abdomen fall as you release the air. Make a soft whooshing sound as you exhale.

5. Pause Before the Next Breath:

- Pause for a count of 2 before taking your next breath. This allows your body to settle into a relaxed rhythm.

6. Repeat the Cycle:

- Continue this cycle of breathing: inhale for 4 counts, hold for 4 counts, exhale for 6 counts, and pause for 2 counts. Repeat for 5-10 minutes.

7. End with Deep Breathing:

- As you finish, take a few final deep breaths at your own pace. Notice how your body feels more relaxed and your mind calmer.

* * *

4-7-8 Breathing Technique

The 4-7-8 breathing technique is a simple but powerful practice that can help stimulate the vagus nerve, reduce stress, and promote relaxation.

1. Place the Tip of Your Tongue:

- Place the tip of your tongue against the ridge of tissue just behind your upper front teeth. Keep it there throughout the entire breathing exercise.

2. Exhale Completely:

- Begin by exhaling completely through your mouth, making a whooshing sound.

3. Inhale Through Your Nose for 4 Counts:

- Close your mouth and inhale quietly through your nose to a mental count of 4. Feel your abdomen rise as you fill your lungs with air.

4. Hold Your Breath for 7 Counts:

- Hold your breath for a count of 7. This brief pause allows your body to fully absorb the oxygen.

5. Exhale Completely Through Your Mouth for 8 Counts:

- Exhale completely through your mouth, making a whooshing sound to a count of 8. Feel your abdomen fall as you release the air.

6. Repeat the Cycle:

- Repeat the cycle for four breaths. Gradually increase to eight breaths over time.

7. Finish with Deep Breathing:

- After completing the cycles, take a few final deep breaths at your own pace. Notice how your body feels more relaxed and your mind calmer.

Alternate Nostril Breathing

1. Position Your Right Hand:

- With your right hand, fold the index and middle fingers toward the palm, leaving the thumb, ring finger, and little finger extended.

2. Close Your Right Nostril:

- Use your right thumb to gently close your right nostril.

3. Inhale Through Your Left Nostril:

- Breathe in slowly and deeply through your left nostril. Focus on filling your lungs completely.

4. Close Your Left Nostril:

- At the end of the inhale, use your right ring finger to gently close your left nostril. Both nostrils are now briefly closed.

5. Open Your Right Nostril and Exhale:

- Release your right thumb and exhale slowly and completely through your right nostril.

6. Inhale Through Your Right Nostril:

- Keeping your left nostril closed, breathe in slowly and deeply through your right nostril.

7. Close Your Right Nostril:

- At the end of the inhale, use your right thumb to gently close your right nostril. Both nostrils are now briefly closed.

8. Open Your Left Nostril and Exhale:

- Release your right ring finger and exhale slowly and completely through your left nostril.

9. Repeat the Cycle:

- This completes one full cycle. Repeat the process for 5-10 minutes, maintaining a steady and relaxed rhythm.

10. End with Deep Breathing:

- After completing the cycles, take a few final deep breaths through both nostrils at your own pace. Notice how your body feels more balanced and your mind calmer.

* * *

Diaphragmatic Breathing

Diaphragmatic breathing, also known as abdominal or belly breathing, is a technique that helps activate the vagus nerve, promoting relaxation and reducing stress.

1. Place Your Hands:

- Place one hand on your upper chest and the other on your abdomen, just below your ribcage. This will help you feel the movement of your diaphragm as you breathe.

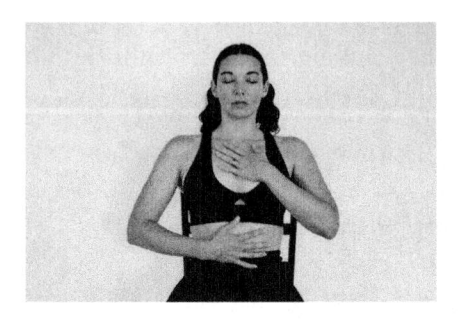

2. Focus on Your Breath:

- Close your eyes to minimize distractions and focus on your breathing. Take a moment to notice your natural breath without trying to change it.

3. Inhale Deeply:

- Breathe in slowly through your nose, allowing the air to move down into your abdomen. You should feel your stomach rise as your diaphragm moves down to make space for the incoming air. The hand on your chest should remain relatively still, while the hand on your abdomen should rise.

4. Pause:

- Hold your breath briefly (1-2 seconds) if it feels comfortable.

5. Exhale Slowly:

- Breathe out slowly through your mouth, making a gentle whooshing sound. Feel your abdomen fall as your diaphragm pushes the air out. The hand on your chest should remain still, while the hand on your abdomen should fall.

6. Repeat the Process:

- Continue this deep breathing cycle. Aim for 5-10 minutes of practice. Start with shorter sessions if needed and gradually increase the duration as you become more comfortable with the technique.

Valsalva Maneuver

The Valsalva maneuver involves exhaling against a closed airway, which can stimulate the vagus nerve and help regulate heart rate.

Note: Consult a healthcare professional before attempting the Valsalva maneuver, especially if you have a heart condition or other health concerns.

1. Take a Deep Breath:

- Inhale deeply through your nose, filling your lungs completely with air.

2. Close Your Airway:

- Close your mouth and pinch your nose shut with your fingers to prevent air from escaping.

3. Bear Down:

- Exhale forcefully as if trying to blow air out, but keep your mouth and nose closed so no air can escape.
- Maintain this pressure for 10-15 seconds, or however long is comfortable.

4. Release the Pressure:

- Release the breath by unpinching your nose, opening your mouth, and then breathing normally.

5. Relax and Breathe Normally:

- Take a few moments to breathe normally and allow your body to relax.

6. Monitor Your Response:

- Pay attention to how your body feels during and after the maneuver. Stop immediately and seek medical advice if you experience dizziness, chest pain, or any discomfort.

7. Repeat if Necessary:

- Repeat the maneuver after a short rest. It's recommended that you do this no more than three times in a session.

* * *

Partnered Synchronized Breathing

Partnered synchronized breathing involves two people breathing in unison to create a sense of connection, relaxation, and mutual calm. This practice can help reduce stress, promote relaxation, and stimulate the vagus nerve.

1. **Positioning**:

   - Sit facing each other with your backs straight, and shoulders relaxed, or lie down side by side. Ensure you are both comfortable and can see or feel each other's breathing.

2. **Establish a Connection**:

   - If you are sitting, make gentle eye contact with your partner to establish a connection. If you are lying down, place a hand on each other's chest or abdomen to feel the breathing.

3. **Relax Your Body**:

   - Close your eyes if it feels comfortable, and take a moment to relax your body, letting go of any tension in your shoulders, neck, and jaw.

4. **Inhale Deeply**:

   - Both partners take a slow, deep breath through the nose, filling the lungs. Allow your abdomen to rise as you inhale.

5. **Exhale Slowly**:

   - Exhale slowly through the mouth, feeling your body relax with each breath. Repeat this deep breathing for 1-2 minutes to synchronize your breathing patterns.

6. Synchronize Your Breathing:

- Lead and Follow: Decide who will lead the breathing initially. The leader starts by inhaling deeply, and the follower synchronizes their breathing with the leader.

7. Breathe in Unison:

- Inhale slowly and deeply together, feeling the rise of your abdomen or chest. Focus on matching the timing and depth of your breath with your partner's.
- Exhale slowly and fully together, maintaining the synchronization. Continue to focus on matching the breath rhythm.

8. Maintain the Synchronization:

- Continue the cycle of synchronized breathing for 5-10 minutes or as long as feels comfortable. Maintain a steady and relaxed rhythm, focusing on the connection and the mutual calm it brings.

9. Focus on Relaxation:

- Pay attention to the sensations in your body and the connection with your partner. If your mind wanders, gently bring it back to the synchronized breath and the present moment.

10. Return to Individual Breathing:

- After completing the desired duration, gradually return to your individual breathing patterns. Take a few deep breaths at your own pace.

11. Reflect on the Experience:

- Reflect on how you feel after the synchronized breathing exercise. Notice any changes in your stress or anxiety levels and acknowledge the sense of calm and connection with your partner.

12. Share Your Experience:

- Take a moment to discuss the experience with your partner. Share any thoughts, feelings, or sensations that arose during the practice.

13. Express Gratitude:

- Express gratitude towards each other for participating in the exercise and creating a calming and supportive environment.

VAGUS NERVE POSES

Tips for Effective Vagus Nerve Poses

Practice Regularly:

- Practice poses daily, even if just for a few minutes, to build the habit and experience its benefits.

Use a Yoga Mat:

- Use a yoga mat or a soft surface for added comfort.

Create a Quiet Environment:

- If possible, eliminate distractions during the practice. This helps you concentrate on the experience and enhances the relaxation benefits.

Combine with Deep Breathing:

- Pair poses with deep breathing techniques to further stimulate the vagus nerve and promote relaxation.

Use Positive Intentions:

- Before starting the practice, set a positive intention, such as releasing stress, finding calm, or cultivating relaxation.

Move Slowly and Mindfully:

- Perform each movement slowly and mindfully, focusing on the stretch and your breath. Avoid forcing your body into the pose.
- Be gentle with yourself and allow the practice to develop naturally. Avoid forcing the movements by letting them flow naturally.

Focus on Your Breath:

- Maintain a steady and relaxed breathing pattern throughout the exercise. Breathe deeply and fully, coordinating your breath with your movements.

Stay Relaxed:

- Keep your body relaxed and your mind calm. Release any tension in your muscles and joints as you move.

Listen to Your Body:

- Pay attention to how your body feels. Adjust the position or stop and rest if you experience any discomfort or pain.

Stay Present:

- Focus on the sensations in your body. If your mind wanders, gently bring it back to the sensation and your breath.

Benefits of Vagus Nerve Poses

Stimulates the Vagus Nerve:

- The combination of flowing movements and deep breathing activates the parasympathetic nervous system, promoting relaxation and reducing stress.

Reduces Anxiety and Stress:

- Helps manage anxiety and stress by calming the mind and body.

Promotes Overall Relaxation:

- Encourages a state of calm and well-being.

Improves Flexibility and Strength:

- Enhances flexibility and strengthens the entire body.

Enhances Mindfulness:

- Brings awareness to the present moment and improves concentration.

* * *

Bridge Pose

The Bridge Pose helps open the chest, stretch the spine, and stimulate the vagus nerve. It can also improve flexibility and relieve tension in the back and neck. If you find it difficult to maintain the pose, use a yoga block or bolster under your sacrum for support.

1. Starting Position:

- Lie flat on your back with your knees bent and your feet flat on the floor, hip-width apart. Place your arms alongside your body with your palms facing down.

2. Foot Placement:

- Ensure your feet are parallel and positioned close enough to your hips that you can touch your heels with your fingertips.

3. Align Your Body:

- Keep your knees and feet aligned, and avoid letting your knees splay out to the sides. Engage your core muscles to support your lower back.

4. Lift Your Hips:

- As you inhale, press firmly into your feet and lift your hips towards the ceiling. Keep your thighs and feet parallel.

5. Lift Your Chest:

- Continue to lift your hips while rolling your shoulders underneath you. Lift your chest towards your chin without moving your chin towards your chest. Your weight should be supported by your feet, shoulders, and arms.

6. Clasp Your Hands (Optional):

- If comfortable, clasp your hands underneath your back and press your arms into the mat to help lift your hips higher.

7. Maintain the Position:

- Hold the Bridge Pose for 15-30 seconds, or as long as is comfortable.
- Continue to breathe deeply and evenly, focusing on expanding your chest with each inhale and releasing tension with each exhale.

8. Release the Pose:

- As you exhale, slowly lower your hips to the starting position. Unclasp your hands and bring your arms back alongside your body.

9. Rest in Supine Position:

- Lie flat on your back with your legs extended and your arms resting by your sides. Close your eyes, take a few moments to relax, and notice the effects of the pose.

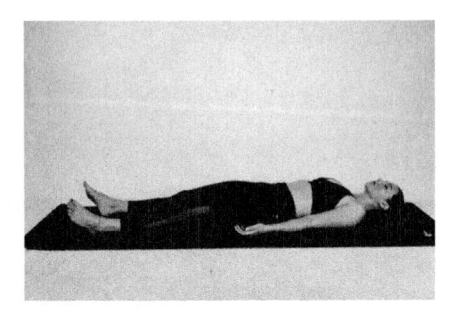

10. Notice Changes:

- Reflect on how you feel after the Bridge Pose. Notice any changes in your stress or anxiety levels and acknowledge the sense of calm and openness in your body.

11. Stay Relaxed:

- Take a moment to sit or lie quietly and enjoy the relaxation and openness in your body.

* * *

Sun Salutation

The Sun Salutation is a series of poses performed in a sequence to create a flow of movement. Performing Sun Salutations can help stimulate the vagus nerve, reduce stress, and enhance overall well-being.

1. Starting Position:

- Stand with your feet together, arms relaxed at your sides, and your weight evenly distributed on both feet.

2. Mountain Pose:

- Stand tall with your feet together. Bring your palms together in front of your chest in a prayer position.

3. Upward Salute:

- Inhale: Sweep your arms out to the sides and then up overhead, reaching toward the sky. Look up at your hands and gently arch your back.

4. Standing Forward Bend:

- Exhale: Hinge at your hips and fold forward, bringing your hands toward the floor. Keep your knees slightly bent if needed. Allow your head to hang heavy and relax your neck.

5. Halfway Lift:

- Place your fingertips on the floor or on your shins. Inhale and lift your torso halfway up, extending your spine and looking forward.

6. Plank Pose:

- Plant your hands on the floor and step back into a plank position. Keep your body straight from head to heels, engaging your core.

VAGUS NERVE EXERCISES 113

7. Four-Limbed Staff Pose:

- Lower your body halfway to the floor, keeping your elbows close to your sides. Engage your core and keep your body straight.

8. Upward-Facing Dog:

- Inhale: Press into your palms, straighten your arms, and lift your chest and thighs off the floor. Open your chest and look slightly upward.

9. Downward-Facing Dog:

- Exhale: Lift your hips up and back, forming an inverted V shape with your body. Press your hands firmly into the mat and extend your spine. Hold this position for five breaths.

10. Halfway Lift:

- Inhale: Step or jump your feet forward between your hands. Lift your torso halfway up, extending your spine and looking forward.

11. Standing Forward Bend:

- Exhale: Fold forward again, bringing your hands towards the floor. Allow your head to hang heavy and relax your neck.

12. Upward Salute:

- Inhale: Sweep your arms out to the sides and then up overhead, reaching toward the sky. Look up at your hands and gently arch your back.

13. Mountain Pose:

- Exhale: Bring your palms together in front of your chest in a prayer position and return to the starting position.

14. Repeat the Sequence:

- Repeat the Sun Salutation sequence for 5-10 cycles, or as long as feels comfortable.

15. Stay Relaxed:

- Pay attention to how your body feels as you continue the Sun Salutations. Notice the relaxation spreading through your body with each movement and breath.

16. Gradually Slow Down:

- After completing the desired number of cycles, gradually slow down the pace of your movements. Take a few deep breaths at your own pace.

17. Rest for a Moment:

- Lie down on your back with your arms by your sides and your legs extended. Close your eyes, rest for a few minutes, and integrate the relaxation and calmness you have cultivated.

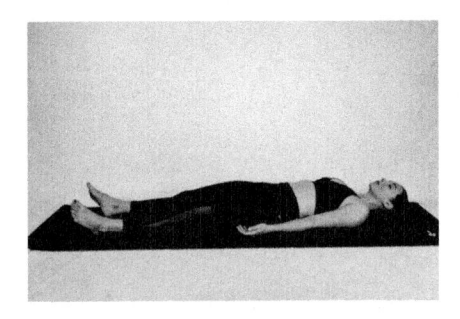

* * *

Seated Forward Bend

The Seated Forward Bend helps stretch the spine, hamstrings, and lower back. This pose can help stimulate the vagus nerve, promote relaxation, and reduce stress. If you cannot comfortably reach your feet, use a yoga strap, towel, or bolster to assist with the stretch. Props can help you maintain proper alignment and avoid straining.

1. Starting Position:

- Sit on the floor with your legs extended straight in front of you. Ensure you are sitting up straight with your spine elongated.

2. Align Your Body:

- Sit with your back straight, shoulders relaxed, and your head aligned with your spine. Flex your feet, keeping your toes pointing towards the ceiling.

3. Take Deep Breaths:

- Take a slow, deep breath in through your nose, filling your lungs completely. Allow your abdomen to rise as you inhale.

4. Raise Your Arms:

- As you inhale, raise your arms overhead, stretching your spine upwards. Keep your arms shoulder-width apart and your palms facing each other.

5. Hinge at the Hips:

- As you exhale, hinge at your hips and begin to fold forward. Keep your spine long and lead with your chest rather than rounding your back.

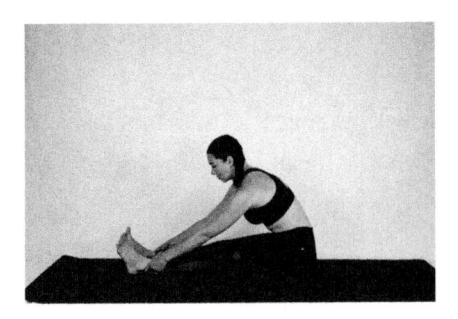

6. Reach for Your Feet:

- Reach for your feet, ankles, or shins—whatever is accessible to you without straining. If you can, hold onto your feet with your hands. If not, use a yoga strap or a towel around your feet to assist.

7. Relax Your Neck and Shoulders:

- Let your head and neck relax, and keep your shoulders away from your ears. Avoid hunching your shoulders.

8. Hold the Pose:

- Hold the pose for 15-30 seconds, or as long as is comfortable. Breathe deeply and steadily, focusing on lengthening your spine with each inhale and deepening the stretch with each exhale.

9. Deep Breathing:

- Continue to take slow, deep breaths throughout the stretch. Inhale deeply through your nose and exhale slowly through your mouth, feeling your body relax with each breath.

10. Slowly Return to the Starting Position:

- As you inhale, slowly lift your torso back to the starting seated position. Bring your arms overhead again, stretching upwards.

11. Lower Your Arms:

- As you exhale, lower your arms back down to your sides.

12. Notice Changes:

- Reflect on how you feel after the stretch. Notice any changes in your stress or anxiety levels and acknowledge the sense of calm and presence.

13. Stay Relaxed:

- Take a moment to sit quietly and enjoy the relaxation and openness in your body.

* * *

Standing Forward Bend

The Standing Forward Bend is a pose that helps stretch the spine, hamstrings, and calves. It can also stimulate the vagus nerve, promote relaxation, and reduce stress. If you cannot reach the floor comfortably, use a yoga block or a chair to support your hands. Props can help you maintain proper alignment and avoid straining.

1. Starting Position:

- Stand with your feet hip-width apart, arms relaxed at your sides, and your weight evenly distributed on both feet.

2. Align Your Body:

- Stand tall with your back straight, shoulders relaxed, and your head aligned with your spine. Engage your core and lift through the crown of your head.

3. Inhale Deeply:

- Take a slow, deep breath in through your nose, filling your lungs completely. Allow your abdomen to rise as you inhale.

4. Raise Your Arms:

- As you inhale, raise your arms overhead, stretching your spine upwards. Keep your arms shoulder-width apart and your palms facing each other.

5. Hinge at the Hips:

- As you exhale, hinge at your hips and begin to fold forward. Keep your spine long and lead with your chest rather than rounding your back.

6. Reach for the Floor:

- Let your hands reach towards the floor. Allow your head to hang heavy and relax your neck.

7. Bend Your Knees Slightly:

- If your hamstrings are tight, bend your knees slightly to avoid straining your lower back. Focus on maintaining a gentle stretch rather than forcing your legs to be straight.

8. Hold the Pose:

- Hold the pose for 15-30 seconds, or as long as is comfortable. Breathe deeply and steadily, focusing on lengthening your spine with each inhale and deepening the stretch with each exhale.

9. Slowly Return to Standing Position:

- As you inhale, place your hands on your hips and slowly lift your torso back to the standing position. Engage your core to support your lower back as you rise.

10. Lower Your Arms:

- As you exhale, lower your arms back down to your sides.

11. Notice Changes:

- Reflect on how you feel after the stretch. Notice any changes in your stress or anxiety levels and acknowledge the sense of calm and presence.

12. Post-Stretch Relaxation:

- Take a moment to stand quietly and enjoy the relaxation and openness in your body.

* * *

Fish Pose

The Fish pose helps stretch the throat, chest, and abdomen, stimulating the vagus nerve and promoting relaxation. It can also help improve posture and relieve tension in the neck and shoulders. If you find it difficult to maintain the pose, use a folded blanket or bolster under your upper back for support.

1. Starting Position:

- Lie flat on your back with your legs extended and your arms resting by your sides.

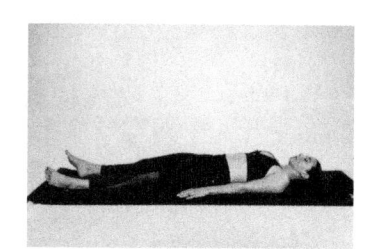

2. Place Your Hands Under Your Hips:

- Slide your hands, palms facing down, under your hips. Keep your elbows close to your body.

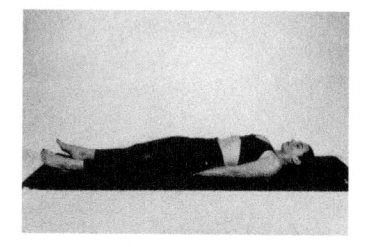

3. Engage Your Core and Legs:

- Press your forearms and elbows into the floor, engaging your core and leg muscles to prepare for the lift.

4. Inhale and Lift Your Chest:

- As you inhale, press firmly into your forearms and elbows to lift your upper body off the mat. Arch your back and lift your chest towards the ceiling.

5. Tilt Your Head Back:

- Gently tilt your head back and rest the crown of your head on the mat. Be mindful not to put too much weight on your head, as most of the weight should be supported by your forearms.

6. Open Your Throat and Chest:

- Open your throat and chest, feeling the stretch along the front of your body. Breathe deeply and evenly.

7. Maintain the Position:

- Hold the Fish Pose for 15-30 seconds, or as long as is comfortable. Continue to breathe deeply and evenly, focusing on expanding your chest with each inhale and releasing tension with each exhale.

8. Lower Your Head and Chest:

- As you exhale, press into your forearms and elbows to lift your head off the mat. Lower your upper body back down to the starting position.

9. Remove Your Hands:

- Slide your hands out from under your hips and rest them by your sides.

10. Rest Position:

- Lie flat on your back with your legs extended and your arms resting by your sides. Close your eyes, take a few moments to relax, and notice the effects of the pose.

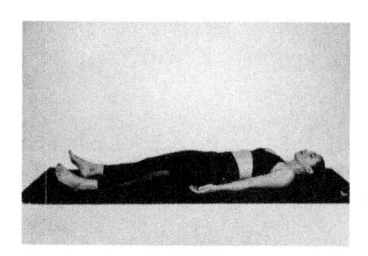

11. Notice Changes:

- Reflect on how you feel after the Fish Pose. Notice any changes in your stress or anxiety levels and acknowledge the sense of calm and openness in your body.

Mountain Pose

1. Stand with Your Feet Together:

- Stand tall with your feet together or slightly apart. Distribute your weight evenly across both feet.

2. Engage Your Thighs and Core:

- Slightly engage your thighs by lifting your kneecaps. Draw your belly button in towards your spine to engage your core.

3. Lengthen Your Spine:

- Imagine a string pulling the crown of your head up towards the ceiling, lengthening your spine. Keep your shoulders relaxed and away from your ears.

4. Relax Your Arms:

- Let your arms hang naturally by your sides, with your palms facing forward.

5. Breathe Deeply:

- Take slow, deep breaths through your nose. Inhale deeply, feeling your chest and abdomen expand, and exhale slowly, feeling them contract.

6. Focus on Your Breath:

- Focus on the sensation of your breath and the feeling of stability and grounding in this pose. Hold for 1-2 minutes.

* * *

Child's Pose

1. Tabletop Position:

- Begin on your hands and knees with your wrists directly under your shoulders and your knees under your hips.

2. Sit Back on Your Heels:

- Slowly sit back on your heels, bringing your big toes together and spreading your knees wide apart.

3. Extend Your Arms Forward:

- Extend your arms forward on the mat, allowing your forehead to rest on the floor. Keep your arms extended, or bring them alongside your body with palms facing up.

4. Breathe Deeply:

- Take slow, deep breaths through your nose. Inhale deeply, feeling your abdomen press against your thighs, and exhale slowly, feeling your body relax.

5. Focus on Your Breath:

- Focus on the sensation of your breath and the feeling of relaxation in this pose. Hold for 1-3 minutes.

* * *

Corpse Pose

1. Lie Down on Your Back:

- Lie flat on your back with your legs extended and arms resting by your sides. Let your feet fall open, and your palms face up.

2. Close Your Eyes and Relax:

- Close your eyes and take a moment to relax your body, letting go of any tension.

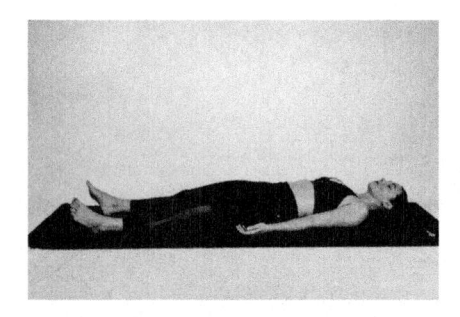

3. **Take a Deep Breath:**

   - Take a slow, deep breath in through your nose, filling your lungs completely, and then exhale slowly through your mouth.

4. **Scan Your Body:**

   - Starting from your toes and moving up to your head, mentally scan your body for any areas of tension. With each exhale, release any tension you find.

5. **Focus on Your Breath:**

   - Focus on the natural rhythm of your breath. Notice the rise and fall of your chest and abdomen with each inhale and exhale.

6. **Stay Present:**

   - Stay in this pose for 5-10 minutes, maintaining a steady, relaxed breathing pattern. Allow your mind and body to relax fully.

Knees-to-Chest Pose

The knees-to-chest pose is a gentle yoga posture that helps to relieve tension in the lower back, improve digestion, and stimulate the vagus nerve. If you find it difficult to hold your knees, use a yoga strap or towel around your shins for support.

1. Lie Down on Your Back:

- Lie flat on your back with your legs extended and arms resting by your sides. Ensure your body is aligned and relaxed.

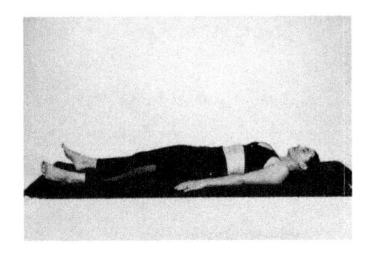

2. Bend Your Knees:

- Bend your knees and gently draw them towards your chest. Use your hands to hold your shins or the backs of your thighs.

3. Adjust Your Hold:

- Clasp your hands around your shins or knees, or use a yoga strap around your shins if it's more comfortable.

4. Relax Your Shoulders and Head:

- Ensure your shoulders are relaxed and your head is resting comfortably on the floor. Avoid tensing your neck or shoulders.

5. Bring Your Thighs Closer:

- Gently draw your thighs closer to your abdomen, feeling a gentle stretch in your lower back and hips. Do not force the movement, as it should be comfortable and relaxing.

6. Focus on Your Breath:

- Close your eyes and focus on your breath. As you inhale, imagine the breath reaching your lower back, and as you exhale, feel the tension releasing from that area.

7. Hold the Pose:

- Depending on your comfort level, stay in the pose for 5-10 deep breaths or up to a few minutes.

8. Rock Gently (Optional):

- If it feels comfortable, gently rock side to side to massage your lower back and further stimulate the vagus nerve.

9. Release the Pose:

- When you are ready to release the pose, slowly lower your feet back to the floor, one at a time, and extend your legs.

10. Rest and Reflect:

- Take a few moments to rest in a neutral position, noticing how your body feels. Reflect on any changes in your stress or anxiety levels and acknowledge the sense of calm and presence.

Cat-Cow

The Cat-Cow is a gentle, flowing pose that helps to increase spine flexibility, relieve tension, and stimulate the vagus nerve.

1. Starting Position:

- Begin on your hands and knees in a tabletop position. Make sure your wrists are directly under your shoulders, and your knees are directly under your hips. Your back should be flat, and your neck should be in a neutral position, gazing at the floor.

2. Align Your Body:

- Spread your fingers wide and press evenly through your hands. Distribute your weight evenly between your hands and knees.

3. Move into Cow Pose:

- As you inhale, drop your belly towards the mat. Lift your chest and tailbone towards the ceiling, creating an arch in your back.
- Gaze up slightly without straining your neck. Keep your shoulders away from your ears.
- Take a deep breath in, expanding your abdomen.

4. **Move into Cat Pose**:

- As you exhale, draw your belly to your spine and round your back towards the ceiling.
- Tuck your chin towards your chest and release your head towards the floor. Your tailbone should be pointing down.
- Engage your hands and knees to create a deep stretch along your spine.

5. **Continue the Flow:**

- Move back into Cow Pose as you inhale, dropping your belly and lifting your chest and tailbone.
- Transition into Cat Pose as you exhale, rounding your back and tucking your chin.
- Continue this flow for 5-10 minutes, synchronizing your breath with each movement.

6. **Focus on Your Breath**:

- Keep your breath smooth and even. Inhale deeply as you move into Cow Pose, and exhale fully as you move into Cat Pose.

7. **Return to Tabletop Position**:

- After completing your cycles, return to a neutral tabletop position with a flat back. Take a few deep breaths here.

8. Rest in Child's Pose:

- Sit back on your heels, stretch your arms forward, and rest your forehead on the mat. To end your exercise, take a few deep breaths in this relaxing pose.

*** * ***

Legs-Up-the-Wall Pose

Legs-Up-the-Wall Pose is a restorative posture that promotes relaxation, reduces stress, and helps stimulate the vagus nerve. If you find it difficult to get your hips close to the wall, use a bolster or folded blanket for additional support under your hips.

1. Starting Position:

- Sit with one side of your body touching the wall. Your knees should be bent, and your feet on the floor.

2. Swing Your Legs Up:

- Gently swing your legs up the wall while lowering your back to the floor. Adjust your position so that your buttocks are as close to the wall as possible and your legs are straight up the wall.

3. Adjust Your Hips:

- If using a bolster or blanket, place it under your hips for support. This will create a slight inversion, which can enhance relaxation.
- Ensure your lower back is comfortable, and your body is in a relaxed position.

4. Position Your Arms:

- Let your arms rest comfortably by your sides, palms facing up. You can also place your hands on your abdomen to feel your breath.

5. Breathe Deeply:

- Close your eyes and take slow, deep breaths. Inhale deeply through your nose, allowing your abdomen to rise, and exhale slowly through your nose or mouth, feeling your body relax.

6. Maintain the Pose:

- Stay in this pose for 5-15 minutes, depending on your comfort level.

7. Release the Pose:

- To come out of the pose, gently bend your knees and slide your feet down the wall.
- Roll onto your side and rest for a moment before slowly sitting up.

8. Relax:

- Sit quietly for a few moments, noticing the effects of the pose on your body and mind.

* * *

Spinal Twists

Yoga spinal twists promote relaxation, improve digestion, and stimulate the vagus nerve. If needed, use a folded blanket or cushion for extra support under your hips or knees.

Seated Spinal Twists

1. Starting Position:

- Sit on the floor with your legs extended straight in front of you. If you need extra support, sit on a folded blanket.

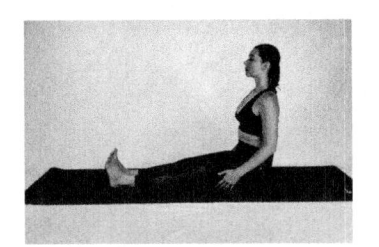

2. Bend Your Right Knee:

- Bend your right knee and place your right foot on the outside of your left thigh. Keep your left leg extended or bend your left knee and bring your left foot near your right hip for a deeper twist.

3. Place Your Right Hand Behind You:

- Place your right hand on the floor behind you for support, keeping your spine straight.

4. Inhale and Lengthen Your Spine:

- As you inhale, lengthen your spine, sitting up tall.

5. Twist to the Right:

- Exhale and twist to the right, bringing your left elbow to the outside of your right knee or hugging your right knee with your left arm.
- Use your right hand to help deepen the twist. Look over your right shoulder, keeping your neck relaxed.

6. Hold the Pose and Breathe:

- Hold the pose for 5-10 breaths, focusing on your breath. Inhale to lengthen the spine and exhale to deepen the twist.

7. Release the Twist:

- Inhale and slowly return to the center, releasing the twist.

8. Switch Sides:

- Repeat the same steps on the other side, bending your left knee and twisting to the left.

Supine Spinal Twists

1. Lie Down on Your Back:

- Lie flat on your back on a yoga mat or a comfortable surface with your legs extended.

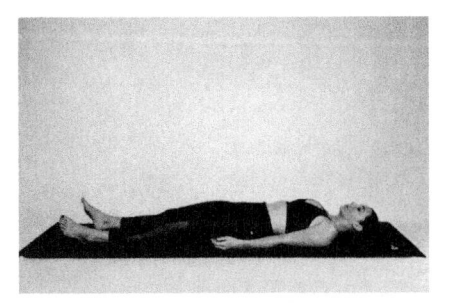

2. Hug Your Knee:

- Bend your right knee and draw it towards your chest. Hug it gently with your hands.

VAGUS NERVE EXERCISES 139

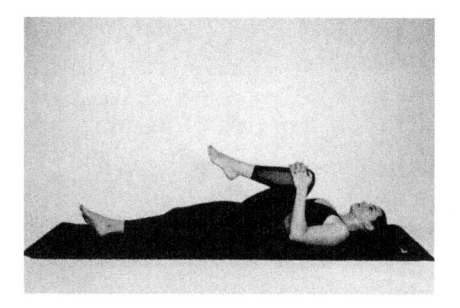

3. Position Your Arm:

- Extend your right arm out to the side at shoulder height, palm facing up. This helps keep your shoulder grounded.

4. Guide Your Knee Across Your Body:

- Use your left hand to gently guide your right knee across your body towards the left side. Allow your knee to move toward the floor.

5. Deepen the Twist:

- Turn your head to the right, looking over your right shoulder. Keep both shoulders grounded as much as possible.

6. Stay in the Twist:

- Hold the pose for 5-10 breaths, focusing on your breath. Inhale to lengthen your spine and exhale to relax deeper into the twist.

7. Release the Twist:

- Inhale and bring your right knee back to the center. Extend your right leg back to the starting position.

8. Switch Sides:

- Repeat the same steps on the other side, bending your left knee and twisting to the right.

* * *

Sphinx Pose

The Sphinx Pose is a gentle backbend that helps to open the chest, strengthen the spine, and stimulate the vagus nerve. If you experience discomfort in your lower back, place a folded blanket or cushion under your pelvis for additional support.

1. Starting Position:

- Lie flat on your stomach, legs extended straight back, feet hip-width apart. Rest your forehead on the mat.

VAGUS NERVE EXERCISES 141

2. Position Your Arms:

- Place your elbows under your shoulders and forearms parallel to each other and to the sides of your mat. Your palms should be flat on the mat, fingers spread wide.

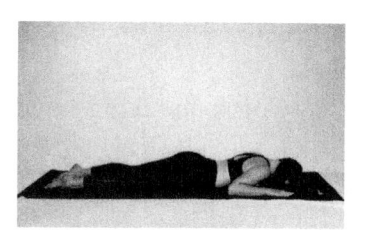

3. Lift Your Chest:

- On an inhale, gently lift your head, chest, and upper abdomen off the mat. Keep your lower ribs, pelvis, and legs grounded.

4. Engage Your Back Muscles:

- Draw your shoulder blades back and down, away from your ears. Engage the muscles of your upper back to support the lift.

5. Lengthen Your Spine:

- Imagine your spine lengthening as you lift your chest. Keep your neck long and gaze forward or slightly downward, ensuring your head is aligned with your spine.

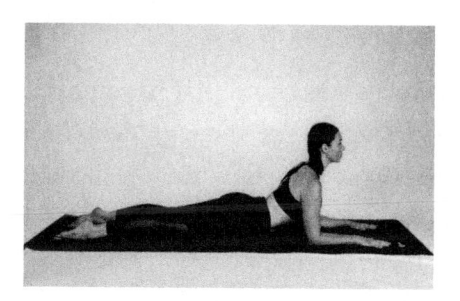

6. Relax and Breathe Deeply:

- Focus on taking slow, deep breaths. Inhale deeply into your abdomen, allowing it to expand, and exhale slowly, feeling the relaxation spread through your body.

7. Hold the Pose:

- Depending on your comfort level, stay in the Sphinx Pose for 5-10 breaths or up to 1-3 minutes.

8. Release the Pose:

- To come out of the pose, exhale and slowly lower your chest and forehead back to the mat. Rest your arms alongside your body and take a few moments to relax.

9. Transition to a Resting Position:

- Turn your head to one side and rest for a few breaths in a prone position. You can also transition to Child's Pose to stretch your back and relax further.

* * *

Easy Pose

Easy Pose is a simple seated pose that promotes relaxation and can help stimulate the vagus nerve through deep breathing and mindfulness. If sitting cross-legged is uncomfortable, use props like cushions or blankets to support your hips and knees. You can also sit against a wall for back support.

1. Sit Down Comfortably:

- Sit on the floor with your legs crossed.

2. Align Your Spine:

- Sit up straight with your spine elongated. Imagine a string pulling the crown of your head towards the ceiling.
- Relax your shoulders away from your ears.
- Rest your hands on your knees or in your lap with your palms facing up or down.

3. Position Your Legs:

- Cross your shins and allow your knees to relax towards the floor. If your knees are higher than your hips, sit on a higher cushion to ensure your hips are above your knees.

4. Close Your Eyes:

- Gently close your eyes to minimize distractions and bring your attention inward.

5. Focus on Your Breath:

- Take a deep breath in through your nose, allowing your abdomen to expand.
- Exhale slowly and completely through your nose, feeling your abdomen fall.

6. Establish a Steady Breathing Rhythm:

- Continue to breathe deeply and evenly, focusing on each inhale and exhale. Aim for a gentle and steady rhythm.

7. Maintain the Pose:

- Stay in Easy Pose for 5-10 minutes or longer if comfortable.

8. Release the Pose:

- Open your eyes gently when you're ready to come out of the pose. Uncross your legs and extend them forward, giving them a gentle shake to release tension.

COLD EXPOSURE

Cold exposure effectively stimulates the vagus nerve, promoting relaxation, reducing inflammation, and enhancing overall well-being.

Tips for Effective Cold Exposure

Consistency:

- Regular practice is key to reaping the benefits of cold exposure. Start with shorter durations and gradually increase as your tolerance builds.

Listen to Your Body:

- Pay attention to how your body responds. If you feel excessively cold, dizzy, or uncomfortable, stop immediately and warm up.

Combine with Breathing Exercises:

- Pair cold exposure with deep breathing exercises to enhance vagus nerve stimulation and relaxation.

Stay Hydrated:

- Ensure you are well-hydrated before and after cold exposure to support your body's response to the cold.

Benefits of Cold Exposure

Stimulates the Vagus Nerve:

- Activates the parasympathetic nervous system, promoting relaxation and reducing stress.

Reduces Inflammation:

- Helps decrease inflammation in the body, supporting recovery and overall health.

Improves Circulation:

- Enhances blood flow and supports cardiovascular health.

Boosts Mood and Energy:

- Increases endorphin levels, improving mood and energy.

* * *

Cold Showers

1. Prepare Yourself Mentally:

- Understand that the initial shock of cold water can be intense. Prepare mentally by acknowledging the benefits of cold exposure.

2. Start with Warm Water:

- Begin your shower with warm water to get comfortable.

3. Transition to Cold Water:

- Slowly turn the water temperature down to cold. Start with a mild cold setting and gradually make it colder.

4. Expose Your Body Gradually:

- Start by letting the cold water hit your feet and hands. Then, move to your arms, legs, and finally, your torso and head.

5. Control Your Breathing:

- Breathe deeply and steadily. Focus on maintaining slow, deep breaths to help manage the shock and discomfort.

6. Stay Under the Cold Water:

- Aim to stay under the cold water for at least 30 seconds to 2 minutes. As you become more accustomed to the cold, you can gradually increase the duration.

7. End with Warm Water (Optional):

- You can end your shower with warm water if you prefer, but finishing with cold water maximizes the benefits.

* * *

Full Immersion in Cold Water

1. Find a Suitable Location:

- Use a bathtub, a cold plunge pool, or a natural body of safe and clean water.

2. Prepare the Cold Water:

- Fill the bathtub or pool with cold water. Add ice cubes if you want to make the water colder, aiming for a temperature between 50-60°F (10-15°C).

3. Acclimate Your Body:

- Sit at the edge of the tub or pool and dip your feet in first. Take a few deep breaths to prepare your body for full immersion.

4. Enter the Water Slowly:

- Gradually lower yourself into the water, allowing your body to adjust to the temperature. Start with your legs, then your torso, and finally, immerse your entire body.

5. Control Your Breathing:

- Focus on slow, deep breaths. Avoid rapid, shallow breathing, which can increase discomfort.

6. Stay Immersed:

- Aim to stay in the cold water for 1-3 minutes. As you become more accustomed, you can extend the duration to 5-10 minutes.

7. Exit the Water Gradually:

- When you're ready to exit, do so slowly. Dry off and warm up gradually with a towel and warm clothing.

Cold Face Splashes

1. Prepare Cold Water:

- Fill a basin or sink with cold water. You can add ice cubes to make it colder.

2. Find a Comfortable Position:

- Stand or sit comfortably near the sink.

3. Hold Your Breath:

- Take a deep breath and hold it before you begin.

4. Splash Your Face:

- Use your hands to splash the cold water onto your face. Focus on the areas around your eyes, forehead, and cheeks.

5. Repeat the Process:

- Splash your face multiple times for about 30 seconds to 1 minute.

6. Dry Your Face:

- Gently pat your face dry with a clean towel.

7. Relax and Breathe:

- Take a few moments to breathe deeply and relax after the cold exposure.

Cold Compresses

1. Prepare the Cold Compress:

- Use a cold gel pack, a bag of ice, or a cloth soaked in ice-cold water. Ensure the compress is at a comfortable, cold temperature but not so cold that it causes discomfort.

2. Find a Comfortable Position:

- Sit or lie in a comfortable position to relax for a few minutes.

3. Apply the Cold Compress:

- Place the cold compress on the back of your neck, across your forehead, or on your chest. These areas are effective for stimulating the vagus nerve.

4. Hold the Compress in Place:

- Hold the compress in place for about 5-10 minutes. Focus on relaxing and taking deep breaths while the cold compress is applied.

5. Remove the Compress:

- After 5-10 minutes, remove the cold compress. After a short break, you can repeat the process if desired.

6. **Relax and Warm Up**:

- Take a few moments to relax and warm up naturally after using the cold compress.

*　*　*

Minimally Clothed Exposure to Cold Weather

1. **Choose an Appropriate Location**:

- Find a safe and controlled outdoor environment with cold temperatures, such as your backyard or a nearby park. Ensure it's safe and free from hazards.

2. **Dress Minimally**:

- Wear minimal clothing, such as shorts and a T-shirt, or just a swimsuit. Make sure you have warm clothing available nearby for when you finish.

3. **Prepare Mentally**:

- Prepare yourself mentally for the cold exposure. Understand that the initial shock may be intense, but focus on the benefits.

4. **Step Outside**:

- Step outside into the cold weather. Start by standing still for a few moments to acclimate to the cold.

5. Move Slowly:

- Slowly walk around or perform gentle movements to keep your blood circulating. Avoid strenuous activity that could lead to excessive sweating.

6. Control Your Breathing:

- Focus on slow, deep breaths. Maintain steady breathing to help your body adapt to the cold.

7. Stay Outside for a Short Duration:

- Start with short durations, such as 1-3 minutes. As you become more comfortable, gradually increase the time spent in the cold.

8. Return Inside and Warm Up:

- When you're ready to finish, return inside immediately and put on warm clothing. You can use a blanket, drink a warm beverage, or take a warm shower to restore your body temperature.

GARGLING

Gargling with water is a simple yet effective technique that can stimulate the vagus nerve, promoting relaxation and reducing stress.

Tips for Effective Gargling

Stay Relaxed:

- Keep your body relaxed while gargling. Tension in your muscles can make the process uncomfortable.

Be Gentle:

- Gargle gently to avoid straining your throat. The goal is to create a soothing vibration, not to forcefully expel air.

Use Saltwater for Added Benefits:

- You can add a pinch of salt to the lukewarm water to help soothe a sore throat and kill bacteria.

Practice Regularly:

- Incorporate gargling into your daily routine, such as after brushing your teeth, to make it a habit.

Mindfulness:

- Focus on the sensation of the water and the sound of your gargling. This can enhance the calming effect and make the practice more meditative.

Benefits of Gargling with Water

Stimulates the Vagus Nerve:

- The vibrations from gargling can activate the vagus nerve, promoting relaxation and reducing stress.

Soothes the Throat:

- Gargling can help alleviate throat discomfort and clear mucus.

Improves Oral Hygiene:

- Regular gargling can help reduce mouth bacteria and improve oral health.

Enhances Digestion:

- Gargling can promote better digestion and gut health by stimulating the vagus nerve.

* * *

Gargling Step-by-Step

1. Prepare Your Water:

- Fill a glass with clean, lukewarm water. Lukewarm water is generally more comfortable to gargle with than cold or hot water.

2. Choose a Comfortable Location:

- Stand or sit near a sink, as you must spit out the water after gargling.

3. Take a Sip of Water:

- Take a small sip of lukewarm water into your mouth. To prevent choking, avoid taking too much water at once.

4. Tilt Your Head Back:

- Tilt your head back slightly so that the water moves to the back of your throat without swallowing it.

5. Gargle:

- Action: Open your mouth slightly and exhale gently to create a gargling sound. Try to maintain a consistent gargling sound by keeping the back of your throat open.
- Duration: Gargle for about 15-30 seconds, or as long as is comfortable.

6. Spit Out the Water:

- After gargling, spit the water out into the sink.

7. Repeat if Necessary:

- You can repeat the process a few times if desired. Typically, 2-3 rounds of gargling are sufficient to stimulate the vagus nerve.

PROGRESSIVE MUSCLE RELAXATION

Progressive Muscle Relaxation (PMR) is a technique that involves tensing and then relaxing different muscle groups in the body. It helps to reduce stress, promote relaxation, and stimulate the vagus nerve.

Tips for Effective Progressive Muscle Relaxation

Practice Regularly:

- Incorporate PMR into your daily routine to enhance its benefits. Regular practice helps build the habit and improves relaxation.

Use a Calm Environment:

- Choose a quiet, comfortable place where you won't be disturbed. Dim the lights and remove any distractions.

Stay Mindful:

- Focus on the sensations in your body as you tense and release each muscle group. Mindfulness enhances the relaxation effect.

Combine with Deep Breathing:

- Pair PMR with deep breathing exercises to further stimulate the vagus nerve and promote relaxation.

Listen to Guided PMR:

- If possible, use guided PMR recordings to help you through the process, especially when you're first starting.

Benefits of Progressive Muscle Relaxation

Stimulates the Vagus Nerve:

- Activates the parasympathetic nervous system, promoting relaxation and reducing stress.

Reduces Muscle Tension:

- Helps release physical tension in the muscles, alleviating discomfort and promoting relaxation.

Enhances Mindfulness:

- Encourages awareness of the body and present-moment sensations.

Improves Sleep:

- Regular practice can improve sleep quality by promoting a state of calm before bedtime.

Lowers Stress and Anxiety:

- Reduces overall stress and anxiety levels by calming the mind and body.

Progressive Muscle Relaxation Step-by-Step

1. **Find a Comfortable Position**:

   - Lie Down or Sit Comfortably: Choose a quiet place where you won't be disturbed. Lie on a bed or a mat, or sit comfortably in a chair with your feet flat on the floor.

2. **Close Your Eyes and Breathe Deeply**:

   - Take a few deep breaths, inhaling slowly through your nose and exhaling through your mouth. Focus on your breath and let go of any tension.

3. **Start with Your Feet**:

   - Tense Your Feet: Curl your toes tightly and hold the tension for 5-10 seconds.
   - Release: Slowly release the tension and notice the relaxation in your feet.

4. **Move Up to Your Calves**:

   - Tense Your Calves: Flex your feet downwards, tightening your calf muscles. Hold for 5-10 seconds.
   - Release: Slowly release the tension and feel the relaxation spread through your calves.

5. **Focus on Your Thighs**:

   - Tense Your Thighs: Squeeze your thigh muscles tightly. Hold for 5-10 seconds.

- Release: Gradually release the tension and notice the sensation of relaxation.

6. Tense Your Buttocks:

- Tense Your Buttocks: Squeeze your buttocks muscles together tightly. Hold for 5-10 seconds.
- Release: Release the tension and feel the relaxation in your buttocks.

7. Move to Your Abdomen:

- Tense Your Abdomen: Suck in your stomach muscles tightly. Hold for 5-10 seconds.
- Release: Let go of the tension and feel the relaxation in your abdomen.

8. Focus on Your Hands:

- Tense Your Hands: Clench your fists tightly. Hold for 5-10 seconds.
- Release: Open your hands and feel the relaxation in your fingers and hands.

9. Flex Your Arms:

- Flex Your Arms: Bend your elbows and tense your biceps. Hold for 5-10 seconds.
- Release: Slowly release the tension and feel the relaxation spread through your arms.

10. Tense Your Shoulders and Neck:

- Tense Your Shoulders: Shrug your shoulders up towards your ears tightly. Hold for 5-10 seconds.
- Release: Slowly lower your shoulders and feel the relaxation.

11. Focus on Your Face:

- Tense Your Face: Scrunch your facial muscles tightly, including your forehead, eyes, nose, and mouth. Hold for 5-10 seconds.
- Release: Gradually release the tension and feel the relaxation in your facial muscles.

12. Finish with Your Whole Body:

- Take a moment to scan your entire body from head to toe. Notice any remaining areas of tension and imagine them melting away as you breathe deeply.

13. Breathe Deeply and Relax:

- Continue to breathe deeply and enjoy the sensation of relaxation throughout your body. Stay in this relaxed state for a few minutes, focusing on your breath and the feeling of calm.

HUMMING

Tips for Effective Humming

Practice Regularly:

- Consistency is key. Practice humming daily, even if just for a few minutes, to build the habit and experience its benefits.

Create a Relaxing Environment:

- Find a quiet place where you won't be disturbed. Dim the lights and remove any distractions to help you focus on the humming and its vibrations.

Use Gentle Pressure:

- Hum softly and gently. The goal is to create a soothing vibration, not to strain your vocal cords.

Combine with Breathing Exercises:

- Pair humming with deep breathing exercises to further stimulate the vagus nerve and promote relaxation.

Stay Comfortable:

- Ensure you are in a comfortable position throughout the practice. Adjust your posture if needed to avoid any discomfort.

Benefits of Humming

Stimulates the Vagus Nerve:

- Activates the parasympathetic nervous system, promoting relaxation and reducing stress.

Reduces Anxiety and Stress:

- Calms the mind and body, helping to manage anxiety and stress.

Improves Focus and Concentration:

- Helps clear the mind and enhance mental clarity.

Promotes Overall Relaxation:

- Encourages a state of calm and well-being.

Enhances Respiratory Efficiency:

- Strengthens the diaphragm and improves lung function.

* * *

Humming Step-by-Step

1. Find a Comfortable Position:

- Choose a quiet, comfortable place. Sit in a chair with your back straight and feet flat on the floor, or lie on your back on a bed or mat with your arms by your sides.

2. Close Your Eyes and Relax:

- Close your eyes to minimize distractions. Take a moment to relax your body, letting go of any tension.

3. Take a Deep Inhale:

- Breathe in slowly and deeply through your nose, filling your lungs completely and allowing your abdomen to rise.

4. Exhale with a Hum:

- As you exhale, close your lips and hum softly. Focus on creating a steady, gentle humming sound. Feel the vibration in your chest, throat, and head.

5. Focus on the Vibration:

- Pay attention to the soothing vibration created by the humming sound. This vibration helps stimulate the vagus nerve and promotes relaxation.

6. Continue the Cycle:

- After each hum, take another deep inhale through your nose and exhale with a hum. Continue this cycle for 5-10 minutes.

7. Experiment with Pitch and Tone:

- You can experiment with different pitches and tones to find what feels most soothing. Higher pitches create more vibration in the head, while lower pitches are felt more in the chest.

8. End with Deep Breathing:

- Finish: After completing the humming cycles, take a few final deep breaths at your own pace. Notice how your body feels more relaxed and your mind calmer.

Additional Humming Exercises

Bee Breath with Ear Closing

This technique combines humming with the closing of the ears to enhance the vibration and calming effect.

1. Find a Comfortable Position:

- Sit in a chair with your back straight and feet flat on the floor, or sit cross-legged on a cushion or yoga mat. Keep your spine straight and shoulders relaxed.

2. Close Your Eyes and Relax:

- Close your eyes to minimize distractions. Take a moment to relax your body, letting go of any tension.

3. Position Your Hands:

- Place your index fingers gently on your ear cartilage (the flap covering the ear canal) and gently press to close your ears.

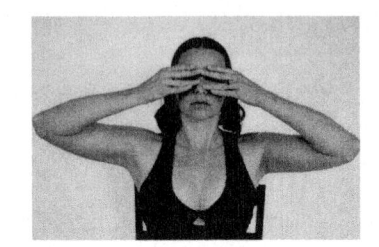

4. Inhale Deeply:

- Take a deep breath in through your nose, filling your lungs completely.

5. Exhale with a Hum:

- As you exhale, close your lips and hum, feeling the vibration in your head. The closed ears amplify the internal sound and vibration.

6. Focus on the Vibration:

- Pay attention to the soothing vibration created by the humming sound. This vibration helps stimulate the vagus nerve and promotes relaxation.

7. Repeat the Cycle:

- Continue this cycle for 5-10 minutes, focusing on the vibration and sound.

8. End with Deep Breathing:

- After completing the humming cycles, take a few final deep breaths at your own pace. Notice how your body feels more relaxed and your mind calmer.

Chanting Om

Chanting the syllable "Om" can create a deep vibration that helps stimulate the vagus nerve.

1. Find a Comfortable Position:

- Sit in a chair with your back straight and feet flat on the floor, or sit cross-legged on a cushion or yoga mat. Keep your spine straight and shoulders relaxed.

2. Close Your Eyes and Relax:

- Close your eyes to minimize distractions. Take a moment to relax your body, letting go of any tension.

3. Inhale Deeply:

- Take a deep breath in through your nose, filling your lungs completely.

4. Chant Om:

- As you exhale, chant the syllable "Om." Start with the sound "Ooo" and gradually move to "Mmm," feeling the vibration in your chest, throat, and head.

5. Focus on the Vibration:

- Pay attention to the soothing vibration created by the chant. This vibration helps stimulate the vagus nerve and promotes relaxation.

6. Repeat the Cycle:

- Continue chanting "Om" for 5-10 minutes, focusing on the vibration and sound.

7. End with Deep Breathing:

- After completing the chanting, take a few final deep breaths at your own pace. Notice how your body feels more relaxed and your mind calmer.

* * *

Humming with Tapping

This technique combines humming with gentle tapping on your chest to enhance the relaxation effect.

1. Find a Comfortable Position:

- Sit in a chair with your back straight and feet flat on the floor, or sit cross-legged on a cushion or yoga mat. Keep your spine straight and shoulders relaxed.

2. Close Your Eyes and Relax:

- Close your eyes to minimize distractions. Take a moment to relax your body, letting go of any tension.

3. Take a Deep Inhale:

- Breathe in slowly and deeply through your nose, filling your lungs completely and allowing your abdomen to rise.

4. Exhale with a Hum:

- As you exhale, close your lips and hum softly. Simultaneously, use your fingertips to gently tap on your chest, just below the collarbones.

5. Focus on the Vibration and Tapping:

- Pay attention to the soothing vibration of the humming sound and the gentle tapping sensation. This combination helps stimulate the vagus nerve and promotes relaxation.

6. Continue the Cycle:

- Continue this cycle for 5-10 minutes, focusing on the vibration and tapping.

7. End with Deep Breathing:

- After completing the humming and tapping cycles, take a few final deep breaths at your own pace. Notice how your body feels more relaxed and your mind calmer.

SINGING

Tips for Effective Singing

Practice Regularly:

- Consistency is key. Practice singing daily, even for a few minutes, to build the habit and experience its benefits.

Create a Relaxing Environment:

- Find a quiet place where you won't be disturbed. Dim the lights and remove distractions to help you focus on the singing and its vibrations.

Sing Naturally:

- Avoid straining your voice. Sing naturally and comfortably, focusing on creating a soothing vibration.

Combine with Deep Breathing:

- Pair singing with deep breathing exercises to further stimulate the vagus nerve and promote relaxation.

Use Relaxing Songs:

- Choose songs that you find calming and enjoyable.

Benefits of Singing

Stimulates the Vagus Nerve:

- Activates the parasympathetic nervous system, promoting relaxation and reducing stress.

Reduces Anxiety and Stress:

- Calms the mind and body, helping to manage anxiety and stress.

Improves Focus and Concentration:

- Helps clear the mind and enhance mental clarity.

Promotes Overall Relaxation:

- Encourages a state of calm and well-being.

Enhances Respiratory Efficiency:

- Strengthens the diaphragm and improves lung function.

Boosts Mood:

- Singing releases endorphins and oxytocin, improving mood and fostering a sense of happiness.

Singing Step-by-Step

1. Find a Comfortable Position:

- Choose a quiet, comfortable place to sit or stand with good posture. If sitting, keep your back straight and feet flat on the floor. If standing, distribute your weight evenly on both feet.

2. Close Your Eyes and Relax:

- Close your eyes to minimize distractions. Take a moment to relax your body, letting go of any tension.

3. Take a Deep Inhale:

- Breathe in slowly and deeply through your nose, filling your lungs completely and allowing your abdomen to rise.

4. Begin Singing:

- Start with a simple song, a vowel sound (like "ah," "ee," or "oo"), or a comfortable pitch. Focus on singing gently and naturally.
- As you exhale, sing your chosen song or tone. Feel the vibrations in your chest, throat, and head.

5. Focus on the Vibration:

- Pay attention to the soothing vibration created by your singing. This vibration helps stimulate the vagus nerve and promotes relaxation.

6. Continue the Cycle:

- After each singing exhale, take another deep inhale through your nose and continue singing. Repeat this cycle for 5-10 minutes.

7. Experiment with Pitch and Tone:

- You can experiment with different pitches, tones, and songs to find what feels most soothing. Higher pitches create more vibration in the head, while lower pitches are felt more in the chest.

8. End with Deep Breathing:

- After completing your singing session, take a few final deep breaths at your own pace. Notice how your body feels more relaxed and your mind calmer.

GUIDED IMAGERY

Guided imagery is a relaxation technique that uses visualizations to create a calming mental image. It helps reduce stress and stimulate the vagus nerve.

Tips for Effective Guided Imagery

Practice Regularly:

- Consistency is key. Practice guided imagery daily, even for a few minutes, to build the habit and experience its benefits.

Create a Quiet Environment:

- Find a quiet place where you won't be disturbed. This will help you focus on your visualization and enhance the relaxation benefits.

Use Guided Recordings:

- If you find it challenging to visualize on your own, use guided imagery recordings or apps to help you through the process.

Stay Patient:

- It may take a few sessions to get comfortable with guided imagery. Be patient with yourself and allow the practice to develop naturally.

Combine with Deep Breathing:

- Pair guided imagery with deep breathing exercises to further stimulate the vagus nerve and promote relaxation.

Benefits of Guided Imagery

Stimulates the Vagus Nerve:

- The calming imagery and deep breathing can activate the parasympathetic nervous system, promoting relaxation and reducing stress.

Enhances Mindfulness:

- Engaging your imagination helps bring awareness to the present moment.

Reduces Anxiety and Stress:

- Shifts attention away from anxious thoughts to a peaceful and calming scene.

Promotes Overall Relaxation:

- Encourages a state of calm and well-being.

Improves Emotional Regulation:

- Helps you become more aware of your emotions and respond to them more effectively.

* * *

Guided Imagery Step-by-Step

1. Choose a Comfortable Location:

- Select a quiet, comfortable place to sit or lie down without disturbances. If sitting, keep your back straight and feet flat on the floor. If lying down, rest comfortably on your back with your arms by your sides.

2. **Close Your Eyes and Relax**:

- Prepare for Visualization: Close your eyes to minimize distractions. Take a moment to relax your body, letting go of any tension in your shoulders, neck, and jaw.

3. **Deep Breathing**:

- Inhale and Exhale: Take slow, deep breaths through your nose. Inhale deeply, allowing your abdomen to rise, and exhale slowly through your mouth, feeling your body relax with each breath.

4. **Choose a Peaceful Scene**:

- Imagine a place where you feel completely relaxed and at peace. This could be a beach, a forest, a garden, or any other place that brings you comfort and calm.

5. **Engage All Your Senses**:

- Sight: Visualize the colors, shapes, and objects in your peaceful place. What do you see around you?
- Sound: Imagine the sounds in your peaceful place. Do you hear birds singing, waves crashing, or leaves rustling?
- Smell: Notice any scents in the air. Can you smell the fresh ocean breeze, flowers, or pine trees?
- Touch: Feel the textures around you. What does the ground feel like under your feet? Is there a gentle breeze on your skin?
- Taste: If applicable, imagine any tastes that might be present in your peaceful place, like the salty air of the sea or the fresh taste of fruit.

6. Focus on Details:

- Immerse yourself fully in the scene, focusing on the details. Imagine walking around and exploring your peaceful place. Notice how you feel as you take in the sights, sounds, smells, and textures.

7. Stay Present:

- Keep your focus on the present moment within your visualization. If your mind wanders, gently bring it back to your peaceful scene.

8. Breathe Deeply:

- Continue to take slow, deep breaths as you immerse yourself in the visualization. With each inhale, imagine drawing in peace and calm; with each exhale, release any tension or stress.

9. Hold the Image:

- Stay in your peaceful place for 5-10 minutes or as long as feels comfortable.

10. Gradually Return:

- Take a few deeper breaths when you are ready to end the visualization. Slowly bring your awareness back to your surroundings.

11. Open Your Eyes:

- Gently open your eyes and take a moment to notice how you feel. Reflect on any changes in your stress or anxiety levels and acknowledge the sense of calm and presence.

12. Notice Changes:

- Reflect on how you feel after the guided imagery exercise. Notice any changes in your stress or anxiety levels and acknowledge the sense of calm and presence.

MEDITATION

Tips for Effective Meditation

Practice Regularly:

- Consistency is key. Practice mindfulness meditation daily, even for a few minutes, to build the habit and experience its benefits.

Create a Quiet Environment:

- Find a quiet place where you won't be disturbed. Dim the lights and remove any distractions to help you focus.

Be Patient with Yourself:

- It's normal for your mind to wander. Be patient and gently guide your focus back to your breath each time it happens.

Combine with Deep Breathing:

- Pair mindfulness meditation with deep breathing exercises to further stimulate the vagus nerve and promote relaxation.

Use Guided Meditations:

- If you find it challenging to meditate on your own, use guided meditation recordings or apps to help you through the process.

Benefits of Meditation

Stimulates the Vagus Nerve:

- The focus on breathing and relaxation can activate the parasympathetic nervous system, promoting relaxation and reducing stress.

Enhances Mindfulness:

- Brings awareness to the present moment and improves concentration.

Reduces Anxiety and Stress:

- Helps manage anxiety and stress by calming the mind and body.

Promotes Overall Well-Being:

- Encourages a state of calm and well-being.

Improves Emotional Regulation:

- Helps you become more aware of your emotions and respond to them more effectively.

* * *

Mindfulness Meditation

Mindfulness meditation is a practice that involves paying full attention to the present moment without judgment.

1. Find a Comfortable Position:

- Choose a quiet, comfortable place to sit without disturbances. Sit on a chair with your feet flat on the floor, or sit cross-legged on a cushion or yoga mat. Keep your back straight and your hands resting on your lap or knees.

2. Close Your Eyes and Relax:

- Close your eyes to minimize distractions. Take a moment to relax your body, releasing any tension in your shoulders, neck, and jaw.

3. Focus on Your Breath:

- Pay attention to your natural breathing rhythm. Notice the rise and fall of your chest or abdomen with each inhale and exhale. Do not try to control your breath, but simply observe it.

4. Anchor Your Mind:

- Whenever your mind starts to wander, gently bring your focus back to your breath. It's natural for thoughts to arise, so acknowledge them without judgment and let them pass.

5. Practice Mindful Awareness:

- Focus on the present moment. Notice the sensations in your body, the sounds around you, and the feeling of the air on your skin. If your mind drifts to past or future thoughts, gently guide it back to the present.

6. End Your Meditation:

- When you are ready to end your meditation, take a few deeper breaths. Slowly bring your awareness back to your surroundings. Open your eyes gently and take a moment to notice how you feel.

7. Reflect on the Experience:

- Reflect on how you feel after the meditation. Notice any changes in your stress or anxiety levels and acknowledge the sense of calm and presence.

* * *

Loving-Kindness Meditation

Loving-kindness meditation, or Metta meditation, involves cultivating love and compassion towards yourself and others.

1. **Sit Comfortably**:

   - Select a quiet, comfortable place to sit without disturbances. Sit with your back straight and shoulders relaxed. You can sit on a chair with your feet flat on the floor or cross-legged on a cushion.

2. **Relax Your Body**:

   - Close your eyes to minimize distractions. Take a moment to relax your body, releasing any tension in your shoulders, neck, and jaw.

3. **Begin with Self-Love**:

   - Begin by directing loving-kindness towards yourself. Silently repeat the following phrases or similar ones that resonate with you:

     - "May I be happy."
     - "May I be healthy."
     - "May I be safe."
     - "May I live with ease."

4. **Visualization**:

   - Visualize yourself surrounded by a warm, loving light. Feel the warmth and compassion filling your heart and spreading throughout your body.

5. Extend Loving-Kindness to Others:

- Loved Ones:

  - Next, think of someone you love deeply. Silently repeat the following phrases, or similar ones, directed towards them:

    - "May you be happy."
    - "May you be healthy."
    - "May you be safe."
    - "May you live with ease."

- Neutral Persons:

  - Think of someone you feel neutral about, such as a colleague or neighbor. Repeat the loving-kindness phrases for them.

- Difficult Persons:

  - Think of someone with whom you have a difficult relationship. Extend the same loving-kindness phrases to them, acknowledging any resistance and gently letting it go.

- All Beings:

  - Finally, extend loving-kindness to all beings everywhere. Visualize the entire world bathed in loving light and repeat the phrases:

- "May all beings be happy."
- "May all beings be healthy."
- "May all beings be safe."
- "May all beings live with ease."

6. Deep Breathing:

- Throughout the meditation, maintain a steady and relaxed breathing pattern. Inhale deeply through your nose and exhale slowly through your mouth.

7. Stay Present:

- Focus on the sensations and emotions that arise during the meditation. If your mind starts to wander, gently bring it back to the phrases and the feelings of loving-kindness.

8. Gradually Return to Awareness:

- Take a few deep breaths when you are ready to end the meditation. Slowly bring your awareness back to your surroundings.

9. Reflect on the Experience:

- Reflect on how you feel after the meditation. Notice any changes in your stress or anxiety levels and acknowledge the sense of calm and compassion.

10. Rest for a Moment:

- Take a moment to sit quietly and integrate the feelings of loving-kindness and compassion you have cultivated.

***

Body Scan Meditation

Body scan meditation is a mindfulness practice that involves paying systematic attention to different body parts.

1. Find a Comfortable Position:

- Choose a quiet, comfortable place to lie on your back or sit without disturbances. If lying down, rest comfortably with your arms by your sides and your legs slightly apart. If sitting, keep your back straight and your feet flat on the floor.

2. Close Your Eyes and Relax:

- Close your eyes to minimize distractions. Take a moment to relax your body, releasing any tension in your shoulders, neck, and jaw.

3. Take a Deep Breath:

- Take a slow, deep breath in through your nose, filling your lungs completely, and then exhale slowly through your mouth. Focus on the sensation of your breath entering and leaving your body.

4. Begin the Body Scan:

- Start with Your Toes: Bring your attention to your toes. Notice any sensations, whether warmth, coolness, tingling, or pressure. Simply observe without judgment.

- Take a deep breath in and out, imagining the breath reaching all the way to your toes.

5. **Move Up Your Body**:

   - Feet and Ankles: Shift your focus to your feet and ankles. Notice any sensations or areas of tension. Take a deep breath in and out, directing your breath to these areas.
   - Calves and Knees: Move your attention to your calves and knees. Observe any sensations and breathe deeply, sending your breath to these parts of your body.
   - Thighs and Hips: Focus on your thighs and hips. Notice any tightness or relaxation. Breathe deeply, imagining the breath filling your thighs and hips.

6. **Focus on Your Torso**:

   - Lower Back and Abdomen: Bring your attention to your lower back and abdomen. Notice how these areas feel. Take a deep breath in and out, sending your breath to your lower back and abdomen.
   - Upper Back and Chest: Shift your focus to your upper back and chest. Observe any sensations and breathe deeply, imagining the breath reaching your upper back and chest.

7. **Move to Your Arms**:

   - Hands and Wrists: Focus on your hands and wrists. Notice any sensations and take a deep breath in and out, sending your breath to your hands and wrists.
   - Forearms and Elbows: Focus on your forearms and elbows, observing any tension or relaxation. Breathe

deeply, imagining the breath filling your forearms and elbows.
- Upper Arms and Shoulders: Shift your focus to your upper arms and shoulders. Notice how these areas feel. Take a deep breath in and out, directing your breath to them.

8. Focus on Your Neck and Head:

- Neck and Throat: Bring your attention to your neck and throat. Observe any sensations or tension. Breathe deeply, imagining the breath reaching your neck and throat.
- Face and Head: Focus on your face and head. Notice any areas of tightness or relaxation. Take a deep breath in and out, sending your breath to your face and head.

9. Scan Your Entire Body:

- Take a moment to scan your entire body from head to toe. Notice how your body feels as a whole. Breathe deeply, imagining the breath flowing through your entire body.

10. End Your Meditation:

- When you are ready to end your meditation, take a few deeper breaths. Slowly bring your awareness back to your surroundings. Open your eyes gently and take a moment to notice how you feel.

11. Reflect on the Experience:

- Reflect on how you feel after the body scan meditation. Notice any changes in your stress or anxiety levels and acknowledge the sense of calm and presence.

CONCLUSION

As we reach the end of our shared journey through the intricate and fascinating landscape of the vagus nerve, it's important to pause and reflect on the ground we've covered together. From the initial steps of understanding the vital role of the vagus nerve in regulating our body's systems to diving into the transformative exercises, we've navigated complex concepts and made them understandable and actionable in our daily lives.

Throughout this book, we've explored key insights that underscore the vagus nerve's critical role in our overall health. We've learned how this remarkable nerve influences our response to stress and trauma and how it can be a powerful ally in managing conditions like anxiety, depression, and chronic inflammation. By incorporating various practical exercises tailored to address specific health issues, we've seen how possible it is to enhance our mental, emotional, and physical well-being. The potential for transformation when you begin incorporating vagus nerve exercises into your routine is immense. Understanding and optimizing your vagal tone empowers you to take control of aspects of your health that you might have thought were beyond your influence. This empowerment is a central theme of our discussions because you have the capacity to enact real, positive change in your life.

It's crucial to remember that improving vagal tone is an incredibly personal journey. Each exercise and routine can and should be adapted to fit your unique circumstances, preferences, and health objectives. Start small—perhaps integrate one or two exercises into your daily routine. Over time, as you become more comfortable and start to notice the benefits, you can expand your practice. Patience and consistency are your allies here. The rewards, though they accumulate gradually, are worth your dedication.

I encourage you to reach out and share your experiences with others walking a similar path. Building a community, whether online, in local groups, or with friends and family, can significantly enhance your motivation and broaden your understanding. Sharing your journey not only supports your own growth but can also inspire and empower others.

Stay curious and open to new discoveries. The field of vagus nerve health is dynamic, with new research and developments continually emerging. Follow reputable sources to stay informed, and consider consulting with healthcare professionals to deepen your practice safely and effectively.

Thank you sincerely for investing your time and trust in this journey with me. Your commitment to enhancing your health is commendable, and I am grateful to have been a part of it.

As we close, I leave you with a message of hope and encouragement: take control of your health and well-being with confidence. Every small step you take in practicing and integrating the principles we've explored is a leap towards a healthier, more vibrant life. Here's to moving forward with strength, knowledge, and the support of the incredible vagus nerve coursing through you.

KEEPING THE CALM ALIVE

Now that you have everything you need to manage stress, reduce anxiety, and improve your overall well-being through vagus nerve exercises, it's time to share what you've learned and help others find the same support.

By leaving your honest opinion of this book on Amazon, you'll guide other readers who are looking for simple, effective ways to take control of their health. Your review can help them discover the tools they need to feel better, just like you did.

Thank you for being part of this journey. The power of vagus nerve exercises stays alive when we pass on our knowledge – and you're helping me do just that.

Scan the QR code or go to the link below to leave your review on Amazon.

https://www.amazon.com/review/review-your-purchases/?asin=B0DH8JNZM7

REFERENCES

Aaronson, S. T., Sears, P., Ruvuna, F., Bunker, M., Conway, C. R., Dougherty, D. D., Reimherr, F. W., Schwartz, T. L., & Zajecka, J. M. (2017). A 5-Year observational study of patients with Treatment-Resistant Depression treated with vagus nerve stimulation or treatment as usual: comparison of response, remission, and suicidality. *American Journal of Psychiatry, 174*(7), 640–648. https://doi.org/10.1176/appi.ajp.2017.16010034

Breit, S., Kupferberg, A., Rogler, G., & Hasler, G. (2018). Vagus nerve as modulator of the Brain–Gut axis in psychiatric and inflammatory disorders. *Frontiers in Psychiatry, 9*. https://doi.org/10.3389/fpsyt.2018.00044

Caron, C. (2022, June 2). *This Nerve Influences Nearly Every Internal Organ. Can It Improve Our Mental State, Too?* The New York Times. https://www.nytimes.com/2022/06/02/well/mind/vagus-nerve-mental-health.html

Clinic, C. (2024, July 2). *Your vagus nerve may be key to fighting anxiety and stress.* Cleveland Clinic. https://health.clevelandclinic.org/what-does-the-vagus-nerve-do

Fang, Y., Lin, Y., Tseng, W., Tseng, P., Hua, G., Chao, Y., & Wu, Y. (2023a). Neuroimmunomodulation of vagus nerve stimulation and the therapeutic implications. *Frontiers in Aging Neuroscience, 15*. https://doi.org/10.3389/fnagi.2023.1173987

Fang, Y., Lin, Y., Tseng, W., Tseng, P., Hua, G., Chao, Y., & Wu, Y. (2023b). Neuroimmunomodulation of vagus nerve stimulation and the therapeutic implications. *Frontiers in Aging Neuroscience, 15*. https://doi.org/10.3389/fnagi.2023.1173987

Gao, J., Leung, H. K., Wu, B. W. Y., Skouras, S., & Sik, H. H. (2019). The neurophysiological correlates of religious chanting. *Scientific Reports, 9*(1). https://doi.org/10.1038/s41598-019-40200-w

Gazetteterrymurphy, & Gazetteterrymurphy. (2024, February 6). *Research shows working out gets inflammation-fighting T cells moving.* Harvard Gazette. https://news.harvard.edu/gazette/story/2023/11/new-study-explains-how-exercise-reduces-chronic-inflammation/

Gelgec, C. (2021, April 11). *Why Cold Showers are all the Rage — Melbourne Wellbeing Group.* Melbourne Wellbeing Group. https://www.melbournewellbeinggroup.com.au/melbourne-psychology-blog/why-cold-showers-are-all-the-rage

Gerritsen, R. J. S., & Band, G. P. H. (2018). Breath of Life: the respiratory vagal stimulation model of contemplative activity. *Frontiers in Human Neuroscience, 12.* https://doi.org/10.3389/fnhum.2018.00397

Goggins, E., Mitani, S., & Tanaka, S. (2022). Clinical perspectives on vagus nerve stimulation: present and future. *Clinical Science, 136*(9), 695–709. https://doi.org/10.1042/cs20210507

Haseltine, W. A. (2023, August 29). Electrically stimulating the vagus nerve may be able to reverse chronic inflammation. *Forbes.* https://www.forbes.com/sites/williamhaseltine/2023/06/29/electrically-stimulating-the-vagus-nerve-may-be-able-to-reverse-chronic-inflammation/

Jannyca. (2023, October 18). *Stimulate your vagus nerve with these 4 yoga poses and practices.* YogaUOnline. https://yogauonline.com/yoga-health-benefits/yoga-for-stress-relief/stimulate-your-vagus-nerve-with-these-4-yoga-nerve-yoga-poses-and-practices/

Jewell, T. (2023, May 19). *What is diaphragmatic breathing?* Healthline. https://www.healthline.com/health/diaphragmatic-breathing

Laborde, S., Mosley, E., & Thayer, J. F. (2017a). Heart rate variability and cardiac vagal tone in psychophysiological research – recommendations for experiment planning, data analysis, and data reporting. *Frontiers in Psychology, 08.* https://doi.org/10.3389/fpsyg.2017.00213

Laborde, S., Mosley, E., & Thayer, J. F. (2017b). Heart rate variability and cardiac vagal tone in psychophysiological research – recommendations for experiment planning, data analysis, and data reporting. *Frontiers in Psychology, 08.* https://doi.org/10.3389/fpsyg.2017.00213

Laderer, A. (2024a, July 18). 5 vagus nerve exercises to help you chill out. *Charlie Health.* https://www.charliehealth.com/post/vagus-nerve-exercises

Laderer, A. (2024b, July 18). 5 vagus nerve exercises to help you chill out. *Charlie Health.* https://www.charliehealth.com/post/vagus-nerve-exercises

Linking the vagus nerve and gut health. (n.d.). https://wisemindnutrition.com/blog/linking-vagus-nerve-gut-health

Parsley Health. (n.d.). *8 vagus nerve stimulation exercises that help you relax.* https://www.parsleyhealth.com/blog/how-to-stimulate-vagus-nerve-exercises/

Pavlov, V. A., Wang, H., Czura, C. J., Friedman, S. G., & Tracey, K. J. (2003, August 1). *The Cholinergic Anti-inflammatory Pathway: a missing link in neuroimmunomodulation.* PubMed Central (PMC). https://www.ncbi.nlm.nih.gov/pmc/articles/PMC1430829/

Porges, S. W. (2007a). The polyvagal perspective. *Biological Psychology, 74*(2), 116–143. https://doi.org/10.1016/j.biopsycho.2006.06.009

Porges, S. W. (2007b). The polyvagal perspective. *Biological Psychology, 74*(2), 116–143. https://doi.org/10.1016/j.biopsycho.2006.06.009

Professional, C. C. M. (n.d.). *Vagus nerve*. Cleveland Clinic. https://my.cleveland clinic.org/health/body/22279-vagus-nerve

Rawlins, A. (2024, August 1). Vagus nerve stimulation: 5 techniques that really work. *Origin*. https://www.theoriginway.com/blog/vagus-nerve-stimulation-5-techniques-that-really-work

Raypole, C. (2024, January 29). *30 Grounding techniques to quiet distressing thoughts*. Healthline. https://www.healthline.com/health/grounding-techniques

Room, S. (2024, April 1). The Vagus Nerve: a secret weapon for calming your mind and voice. *Susan Room 2023*. https://www.susanroom.com/post/the-vagus-nerve

Schwartz, A. (2019, November 13). *The Vagus Nerve in Trauma Recovery | Dr. Arielle Schwartz*. Arielle Schwartz, PhD. https://drarielleschwartz.com/the-vagus-nerve-in-trauma-recovery-dr-arielle-schwartz/

Srakocic, S. (2023, August 18). *Heart rate variability (HRV): What it means and how to find yours*. Healthline. https://www.healthline.com/health/heart-health/heart-rate-variability-chart

Sutton, J., PhD. (2024a, August 1). *Polyvagal theory explained (& 18 exercises & resources)*. PositivePsychology.com. https://positivepsychology.com/polyvagal-theory/

Sutton, J., PhD. (2024b, August 1). *Polyvagal theory explained (& 18 exercises & resources)*. PositivePsychology.com. https://positivepsychology.com/polyvagal-theory/

Sutton, J., PhD. (2024c, August 1). *Polyvagal theory explained (& 18 exercises & resources)*. PositivePsychology.com. https://positivepsychology.com/polyvagal-theory/

Tavoian, D., & Craighead, D. H. (2023). Deep breathing exercise at work: Potential applications and impact. *Frontiers in Physiology, 14*. https://doi.org/10.3389/fphys.2023.1040091

Team, G. (2024, January 18). *11 tips for a morning routine that supports mental health - GoodTherapy.org therapy blog*. GoodTherapy.org Therapy Blog. https://www.goodtherapy.org/blog/11-tips-for-a-morning-routine-that-supports-mental-health-1022197/

Team, L. (2023, April 7). *Stimulating the Vagus Nerve with HRV Biofeedback - Lief Blog*. Lief Blog. https://blog.getlief.com/hrv-biofeedback-for-the-vagus-nerve/

Vagus Nerve. (2021, October 15). Psychology Today. https://www.psychologytoday.com/us/basics/vagus-nerve

Vagus Nerve Exercises: 4 Ways to Handle stress. (2024, March 15). Apollo Neuro. https://apolloneuro.com/blogs/news/4-vagus-nerve-exercises-to-transform-how-you-handle-stress

Vagus nerve stimulation - Mayo Clinic. (2023, April 18). https://www.mayoclinic.

org/tests-procedures/vagus-nerve-stimulation/about/pac-20384565

Vanneste, S., Martin, J., Rennaker, R. L., & Kilgard, M. P. (2017). Pairing sound with vagus nerve stimulation modulates cortical synchrony and phase coherence in tinnitus: An exploratory retrospective study. *Scientific Reports*, *7*(1). https://doi.org/10.1038/s41598-017-17750-y

Printed in Dunstable, United Kingdom